The Brontës' Christmas

The Brontës' Christmas

THE FESTIVE SEASON IN VICTORIAN ENGLAND

EDITED BY MARIA HUBERT
UPDATED BY ANDREW HUBERT VON STAUFER

First published 1996
This revised and updated edition first published 2024

The History Press
97 St George's Place, Cheltenham,
Gloucestershire, GL50 3QB
www.thehistorypress.co.uk

© The Estate of the late Maria Hubert, 1996, 2024

The right of The Estate of the late Maria Hubert to be identified
as the Author of this work has been asserted in accordance with the
Copyright, Designs and Patents Act 1988.

All rights reserved. No part of this book may be reprinted
or reproduced or utilised in any form or by any electronic,
mechanical or other means, now known or hereafter invented,
including photocopying and recording, or in any information
storage or retrieval system, without the permission in writing
from the Publishers.

British Library Cataloguing in Publication Data.
A catalogue record for this book is available from the British Library.

ISBN 978 1 80399 760 5

Typesetting and origination by The History Press
Printed and bound in Great Britain by TJ Books Limited, Padstow, Cornwall.

Trees for LYfe

Contents

INTRODUCTION	7
THE BRONTËS AT CHRISTMAS	11
THE OLD MAN IN THE CHARIOT	16
CHRISTMAS IN THE COUNTRY 1827	20
THE ISLANDERS	22
THE LEGEND	24
THE HOLLY TREE	29
CHRISTMAS CORRESPONDENCE WITH THE POETS	31
MUSIC ON A CHRISTMAS MORN	37
TABBY'S ICY ACCIDENT	40
CHURCH-DECKING	45
THE SPARKLING BOUGH	46
THACKERAY'S CHRISTMAS CRITICISM	48
THE CHEERFUL HEARTH	50
JUVENILE PARTIES – A REMONSTRANCE CONCERNING THEM	51
CHRISTMAS AT WUTHERING HEIGHTS	56

December	64
A Ball, a Game of Charades and Christmas Baking	66
The Pantomime	76
A Christmas Remembered	78
The Mahogany Tree	80
Christmas Storms and Sunshine	82
Annuals, Albums and Christmas Art	96
The Magic Lantern	102
A Tragic Christmas Tale	103
Charlotte's Last Spice Cake	106
The Wassail Cup of 'Old October'	108
The Great Yorkshire Spice Cake	113
Christmas Customs in Brontë Country	115
The Traditional Festive Board	119
The Christmas Party	123
An Imposter at Christmas	125
A New Year Fête	134
Acknowledgements	142

Introduction

Whereas it is true that a Brontë Christmas was a very austere affair and, in their family, dinner parties would have been virtually unknown, it has to be acknowledged that the society around them was moving on.

By the time that Charlotte died in 1855, the Christmas-card industry was well on its way, following the initial private publishing of Sir Henry Cole's first Christmas card in 1843. The penny post was a success, opening up all sorts of opportunities for the developing and increasingly aspirational Victorian middle class.

The Brontë's home county of Yorkshire was particularly renowned for its traditions and embraced a very jolly Christmas. The county, with its mills and mines, was undergoing something of a social revolution: fortunes were being made and the notion of the 'self-made man', as opposed to one who had inherited wealth, was widely accepted, even if they hadn't yet knocked on the doors of the aristocracy.

Washington Irving's *Bracebridge Hall, or the Humorists: A Medley*, was published initially in 1822, when the Brontë girls were still very young; it was popular, describing a notional country-manor Christmas in all its glory. Twenty-five years on and the stage was set for the introduction of Queen Victoria's Christmas tree via *The Sphere* and *The Illustrated London News*, with the attendant middle-class desire for emulating their social betters. Change was in the air, printing was widely available with steel plates, and a plethora of artists well able to see their work mass produced in newspapers and, indeed, attempts at colour reproduction for the emerging greetings-card market.

Already in Germany, various Christmas decorations were being made, including candle holders for the Christmas tree – the first (albeit large) hand-blown Christmas baubles being sold at first through Coburg market, but soon to be exported. The appetite was already there as the developing and increasingly industrialised retail market was set to explode. The middle classes had disposable income. Victorian entrepreneurs were able to raise capital and exploit the trend.

Much of this would seem to have bypassed the Brontë sisters, but even so their father bought some wooden soldiers for the girls' brother, Branwell, that gave rise to Charlotte's stories based on them, beginning with the *The Twelve Adventurers*, written when she was 13.

They were creative, but the overall feeling is one of austerity. This has to have contrasted greatly with what was going on around them in Yorkshire society at large.

It might be a case of the Reverend Brontë fearing for the morals of his daughters in an increasingly aspirational and materialistic world. He put all his faith in his only son, Branwell, who was destined (or so he thought) for fame and success. In today's environment, the girls would probably be regarded as abused.

All their writings, at least in comparison with their contemporary, William Makepeace Thackeray, are subdued when it comes to celebration. Thackeray was indeed read by Charlotte and they became literary friends, but one wonders what the witty and gregarious Thackeray made of the almost eremitical isolation of Charlotte and her sisters.

He went on to evolve with the changing times, writing a number of satirical articles on the family Christmas later

Introduction

in his life. One can but wonder if the Brontës had survived longer would they have embraced the emerging and sometimes rumbustiously colourful Victorian Christmas.

They were contemporary with Charles Dickens but, sadly, shared little of that gentleman's enthusiasm for the season, which is a pity. One cannot help but get a feeling that the idea of guilt at any form of Christmas celebration suffused the atmosphere of the Reverend Brontë's household.

What is certain is that some of Charlotte's illustrations turned up in published Christmas cards within a decade or two of her death. These were undoubtedly pirated, but everything was up for grabs in the days before copyright laws. Whatever the developing commercial Christmas market had in store for Charlotte and her sisters, one thing is certain: they did not benefit!

Their short lives could have marked the transition from the country Christmas of Austen to the urban goodwill of Dickens. This is one of literature's might-have-beens. Sadly we will never know how much happier their festive season might have become.

Andrew Hubert von Staufer
March 2024

The Brontës at Christmas

MRS GASKELL

It is important to introduce Elizabeth Gaskell into any work on the Brontës, no matter how lightly written it may be. As the first and contemporary biographer of Charlotte Brontë, Mrs Gaskell gave us the first valuable glimpses into the family's private lives, and her biography, *The Life of Charlotte Brontë*, was not to be challenged until 1932 when Messrs Wise and Symington produced a grand four-volume work, based on papers and letters which had gone astray through the family of Charlotte's husband.

On 16 June 1855, shortly after her death in that same year, Charlotte's father sent a letter to Elizabeth Gaskell, who had been a family friend during the latter years, asking her to undertake the writing of a biography. She had been used to writing novels, and perhaps this shows in her approach to the biography, which is very accessible. Her blunt honesty regarding the treatment of the children by their father, comments made by the staff, and defamatory comments about school life, was a source of annoyance, and caused some of these remarks to be withdrawn from the original book. However, it shows better than any the background which spawned such a tragic family: the repression, the frustration and disappointment which may have been instrumental in the dissipation of Branwell, and the rather dour attitudes which appear in many Brontë writings.

The following extract chronicles some of the Brontës' Christmases, which pass with rather less momentum than other events such as visits to London or a summer trip to the sea. Such occasions were described almost ecstatically by comparison. Yet Christmas was a time when all the family travelled to be together, no matter how far away, so the Christmas family gathering had obvious importance to them, but then seems singularly lacking in event, or at any rate, the permitted events were not considered important enough to mention in letters or diaries.

Mrs Gaskell's *Life of Charlotte Brontë* was published in 1857 and gives a clear and contemporary account of the attitudes of the time, as well as the personal family restraints within which the Brontës grew up. She begins her biography by painting a picture of this 'landscape', and drawing on the writings of others to add colour. In the following she uses the text of one Dr Davy, to describe the kind of life Charlotte's mother grew up in, in Cornwall, some decades before:

Visiting then was conducted differently from what it is at present. Dinner parties were almost unknown, except at the annual feasting time. Christmas too, was then a season of peculiar indulgence and conviviality, and a round of entertainments was given, consisting of tea and supper. Excepting at these two periods, visiting was almost entirely confined to tea-parties, which assembled at three-o'clock, and broke up at nine, and the amusement of the evening was commonly round some game of cards, as Pope Joan, or Commerce. The lower class was then extremely ignorant, and all classes were very superstitious; even the belief in witches maintained its ground, and there was an almost unbounded credulity respecting the supernatural and monstrous. There was scarcely a parish in the Mount's Bay that was without a haunted house, or a spot to which some story of supernatural horror was not attached. Even when I was a boy, I remember a house in the best street in Penzance which was uninhabited because it was believed to be haunted, and which young people walked by at night at a quickened pace, and with a beating heart. Amongst the middle and higher classes there was little taste for literature, and still less for science, and their pursuits were rarely of a dignified or intellectual kind. Hunting, shooting, wrestling, cock-fighting, generally ending in drunkenness, and a low state of morals, were naturally associated with it . . .

I have given this extract because I conceive it bears some reference to the life of Miss Brontë . . .

Later, on 19 January 1831, Charlotte is sent to Roe Head School near Kirklees, and in 1835 she goes back there as an assistant teacher. Around this time the school is moved to Dewsbury, where the Brontë girls – Charlotte and Anne – feel the air is not so good. (A later biography by Pinion states that the move was in 1837.) The next extract from Mrs Gaskell's biography refers to the following Christmas, that of 1836:

When the sisters met at home in the Christmas holidays, they talked over their lives, and the prospect which they afforded of occupation and remuneration. They felt it was a duty to relieve their father of the burden of their support, if not entirely, or that of all three, at least that of one or two; and, naturally, the lot devolved upon the elder ones to find some remunerative occupation. They knew that they were never likely to inherit much money . . . But this Christmas of 1836 was not without its hopes, and daring inspirations. They had tried their hands at story-writing, in their miniature magazine long ago; they all of them 'made out' perpetually. They had likewise attempted to write poetry; and had a modest confidence that they had achieved a tolerable success. But they knew they might deceive themselves, and that sisters' judgements of each others' productions were likely to be too partial to be depended upon. So Charlotte, as the eldest, resolved to write to Southey. I believe (from an expression in a letter to be noticed hereafter) that she also consulted Coleridge; but I have not met with any part of that correspondence.

On December 29th her letter to Southey was dispatched; and from an excitement not unnatural in a girl who has worked herself up to the pitch of writing to a Poet Laureate and asking his opinion of her poems, she used some high-flown expressions, which, probably, gave him the idea she was a romantic young lady, unacquainted with the realities of life.

This, most likely, was the first of those adventurous letters that passed through the little post office of Haworth. Morning after morning of the holidays slipped away, and there was no answer; the sisters had to leave home, and Emily to return to her distasteful duties, without knowing whether Charlotte's letter had ever reached its destination.

The Christmas which was known to the Brontë children was not, by all accounts, the Christmas which they enjoyed.

Yorkshire, particularly in the late eighteenth and nineteenth centuries, seemed to be divided on the festivity, and not by any level of social class, but by religion: the same division which separated father from son and wife from husband during Cromwell's Commonwealth era. One half of Yorkshire behaved as if there had never been a hint of reform, with all the joy and merriment of the 'Old Christmas'; the other half fought against all but the meanest acceptance of the birth of Christ as a reason to rejoice.

Throughout their novels, especially Charlotte's, there are almost wistful references to Christmas Charades, Wassail Cups and numerous preparations for 'Old Christmas'. Christmas time is always present, even for little tragedies, as in the tale of the dead lover in *Villette* and the mysteriously abandoned little pupil in Charlotte's last and unfinished novel, *Emma*.

Their own diaries and letters seem to drift over the festive season with little mention, though the family always tried to be together for the Christmas holidays. Did they celebrate the way their characters did, with fine foods and balls? Did they play a game of charades, like the one described so vividly in *Jane Eyre*? Perhaps that will forever remain a mystery along with the identity of Emma!

Maybe the 'guisers' bringing their Christmas songs were discouraged from the parsonage door, along with the little Vessel Maids with their half-Christian half-pagan custom, but the Brontë children would have seen them in such a small close-knit community as the village of Haworth, and known all about the customs to which they were possibly not party. They were probably not allowed to decorate their father's church, but surely would have attended the services there and sung the great Christmas hymns. Some of these are attributed to John Wesley himself and could surely not have been disapproved of. It is difficult to believe that they did not enjoy the Christmas table, guests and other innocent enjoyments of the season, yet Charlotte, who opened her heart to her old school friend Ellen Nussey about everything from a trip to the seaside to proposals of marriage, never once mentions anything resembling a Christmas activity in the Brontë household!

The Old Man in the Chariot

AN EXTRACT FROM 'THE SEARCH AFTER HAPINESS' – JUVENILIA FROM 13-YEAR-OLD CHARLOTTE BRONTË.

The Brontë children amused themselves by inventing numerous fantasy lands, which they turned into plays and 'bed-plays', stories played out under cover of the bedclothes away from the strict discipline of their Aunt Branwell and father. They were influenced by such literature as *Arabian Nights* and *Paradise Lost*. These fantasy adventures appear to have begun in 1826, after their father brought back a gift of twelve soldiers from a trip to Leeds. The event is chronicled by Charlotte herself:

Papa bought Branwell some wooden soldiers at Leeds; when Papa came home it was night, and we were in bed, so next morning Branwell came to our door with a box of soldiers. Emily and I jumped out of bed, and I snatched up one and exclaimed, 'This is the Duke of Wellington! This shall be the Duke!' When I said this, Emily likewise took one up and said it should be hers; when Anne came down, she said one should be hers. Mine was the prettiest of the whole, and the tallest, and the most perfect in every part. Emily's was a grave looking fellow, and we called him, 'Gravey'. Anne's was a queer little thing, much like herself, and we called him, 'Waiting-boy'. Branwell chose his, and called him, 'Buonaparte'.

> Thus began the stories of 'The Twelve Adventurers' by Charlotte. In 1830, when he was 13, Branwell created an elaborate story based on these adventures in which he described Glass City, where the twelve 'Young Men' had their history. In her description of her tale, Charlotte says that it is set in Glass town, and indeed her soldier the Duke of Wellington, and other characters from the children's history appear, though it is not strictly part of that history.
>
> It is reproduced here with Charlotte's own spelling and punctuation. The story is about a nobleman called O'Donell who embarks upon a journey of self-discovery, and meets others on the way. The story takes up where they meet a strange old man whom they persuade to tell his story, although the old man's identity remains a mystery!

I was the son of a respectable merchant in Moussoul. My father intended to bring me up in his own trade but I was idle and did not like it. One day when I was playing in the street a very old man came up to me and asked me if I would go with him. I asked him where he was going. He replied that if I would go with him he would show me very wonderful things. This raised my curiosity and I consented. He imediatly took me by the hand and hurried me out of the city of Moussoul so quickly that my breath was almost stopped and it seemed as if we glided along in the air for I could hear no sound of our footsteps. We continued on our course for a long time till we came to [a] glen surrounded by very high mountains. How we passed over those mountains I could never tell. In the middle of the glen there was a small fountain of very clear water. My conductor directed me to drink of it. This I did and imediatly I found myself in a palace the glory of which far exceeds any description which I can give. The tall stately pillars reaching from heaven to earth were formed of the finest and purest diamonds the pavement skarling with gold and precious stones and the mighty dome made solemn and awful by its stupendous magnitude was of one single emerald. In the midst of this grand and magnificent palace was a lamp like the sun the radience of which made all the palace to flash and glitter with an almost fearful grandeur. The ruby sent forth a stream of crimson light the topaz gold the saphire the intensest purple and the dome poured a flood of deep clear splendour which overcame all the other gaudy lights by its mild triumphant glory. In this palace were thousands and tens of thousands of fairies and geni some of whom flitted among the blazing lamps to the sound of unearthly music which dyed and swelled a strain of wild grandeur suited to the words they sung ...

When they had finished there was a dead silence for about half an hour and then the palace began slowly and gradualy to vanish till it disapeared intirely and I found myself in the glen surounded by high mountains the fountain illuminated by the cold light of the moon springing up in the middle of the valley and stand close by was the old man who had conducted me to this enchanted place. He turned round and I could see that his countenance had an expression of strange severity which I had not before observed. 'Follow me' he said. I obeyed and we began to ascend the mountain. It would be needless to trouble you with a repitition of all my adventures. Suffice it to say that after two months time we arrived at a large temple. We entred it. The interior as well as the outside had a very gloomy and ominous aspect being intirely built of black marble. The old man suddenly seized me and dragged me to an altar at the upper end of the temple

The Old Man in the Chariot

then forcing me down on my knees he made me swear that I would be his servant forever. This promise I faithfully kept notwithstanding the dreadful scenes of magic of which every day of my life I was forced to be a witness. One day he told me he would discharge me from the oath and comanded me to leave his service. I obeyed and after wandering about the world for many years I one evening laid myself down on a little bank by the roadside intending to pass the night there. Suddenly I felt myself raised in the air by invisible hands. In a short time I lost sight of the earth and continued on my course through the clouds till I became insensible and when I recovered from my swoon I found myself lying outside this cave. What may be my future destiny I do not know.'

When the old man had finished his tale O Donell and Delancy thanked him for the relation adding at the same time that they had never heard anything half so wonderful. Then as it was very late they all retired to rest. Next morning O Donell awoke very early and looking round the cave he perceived the bed of leaves on which the old man had lain was empty. Then rising he went out of the cave. The sky was covered with fiery red clouds except those in the east whose edges were tinged with the bright rays of the morning sun as they strove to hide its glory with their dark veil of vapours now all beauty and radience by the golden line of light which streaked their gloomy surface. Beneath this storm portending sky and far off to the westward rose two tremendous rocks whose sumits were enveloped with black clouds rolling one above another with an awful magnificence well suited to the land of wilderness and mountain which they canopied. Gliding along in the air between these two rocks was a chariot of light and in the chariot sat a figure the expression of whose countenance was that of the old man armed with the majesty and might of a spirit.

Christmas in the Country 1827

An extract from *Hone's Yearbook*, 1827, of a typical country Christmas during the period of the Brontës, and in a part of the north not too far away from their home in Haworth.

No-where does the Christmas season produce more heart-inspiring mirth than amongst the inhabitants of Cumberland. With Christmas Eve commences a regular series of 'festivities and merry makings'. Night after night, if you want the farmer or his family, you must look for them anywhere but at home; and in the different houses that you pass at one, two, or three in the morning, should you happen to be out so late, you will find candles and fires still unextinguished. At Christmas every farmer gives two 'feasts', one called 't'ould foaks' neet', which is for those who are married, and the other, 't'young foaks' neet' for those who are single.

Suppose you and I, sir, take the liberty of attending one of these feasts unasked (which by the bye is considered no liberty in Cumberland) and see what is going on. Upon entering the room we behold several card parties, some at 'whist', others at 'loo' (there called 'lant') or any other game that may suit their fancy. Masters and servants, rich and poor, humble and lofty, all mingle together without restraint – all cares forgotten – and each one seems to glory in his own enjoyment and that of his fellow-creatures. Cast your eyes towards the sideboard, and there see that large bowl of punch which the good wife is inviting her guests to partake of, with apples, oranges, biscuits, and other agreeable eatables in plenty. The hospitable master welcomes us and requests us to take seats and join at one of the tables.

In due time, someone enters to tell the company that supper is waiting in the next room. Thither we adjourn, and find the raised and minced pies, all sorts of tarts, and all cold – except the welcomes and entreaties – with cream, ale etc., in abundance; in the midst of all a large Goose pie, which seems to say, 'Come and cut again.'

After supper the party return to the card room, sit there for two or three hours longer, and afterwards make the best of their way home, to take a good long nap, and prepare for the same scene the next night. At these 'feasts', intoxication is entirely out of the question – it never happens.

The Islanders

CHARLOTTE BRONTË

This is a fragment from the introduction, by Charlotte Brontë, of a play devised by the children during the Christmas holidays, 1829. This was entitled 'Tales of the Islanders', and was one of their Little Magazines, of which there were many. 'The Islanders' stories were begun in June 1829, and were in four 'volumes'. Part two was written during the Christmas holidays that year, but the idea was formed two years earlier as per the following explanation by Charlotte:

June 31st. 1829
The play of 'The Islanders' was formed in December 1827, in the following manner. One night, about the time when the cold sleet and stormy fogs of November are succeeded by the snow-storms, and high piercing night winds of confirmed winter, we were all sitting round the warm blazing kitchen fire, having just concluded a quarrel with Tabby, concerning the propriety of lighting a candle, from which she came off victorious, no candle having been produced. A long pause succeeded, which was at last broken by Branwell saying, in a lazy manner, 'I don't know what to do.' This was echoed by Emily and Anne.

Tabby 'Wha ya may go t' bed.'
Branwell 'I'd rather do anything than that.'
Charlotte 'Why are you so glum tonight, Tabby? Oh! suppose we had each an island of our own.'
Branwell 'If we had, I would choose the Island of Man.'
Charlotte 'And I would choose the Isle of Wight.'
Emily 'The Isle of Arran for me.'
Anne 'And mine should be Guernsey.'

We then chose who should be chief men in our islands. Branwell chose John Bull, Astley Cooper, and Leigh Hunt; Emily, Walter Scott, Mr. Lockhart, Johnny Lockhart; Anne, Michael Sadler, Lord Bentinck, Sir Henry Halford. I chose the Duke of Wellington and two sons, Christopher North and Co., and Mr. Abernethy. Here, our conversation was interrupted by the, to us, dismal sound of the clock striking seven, and we were summoned off to bed. The next day, we added many others to our list of men, till we got almost all the chief men of the kingdom. After this, for a long time, nothing worth noticing occurred. In June 1828, we erected a school on a fictitious island, which was to contain 1,000 children. The manner of the building was as follows. The Island was fifty miles in circumference, and certainly appeared more like the work of enchantment than anything real.

The Legend

MRS GASKELL

After the Christmas holidays, Charlotte went in January 1831 as a pupil to a new school, Roe Head. This was run by Miss Wooler, with whom Charlotte kept up a correspondence until she died. The school was near the site of Kirklees Priory, which after the Reformation passed into private hands, and at the time of this story was held by Sir George Armitage.

Kirklees has associations with the Robin Hood legend, being the convent where Maid Marion was supposed to have spent her last days, and where Robin died. Naturally such an ancient site is steeped in its own legends and ghost stories, and in the true tradition of all good Christmas anthologies, here follows the story as told by Mrs Gaskell, Charlotte Brontë's biographer.

Roe Head, a cheerful roomy country house, standing apart in a field, on the right of the road from Leeds to Huddersfield. Two tiers of old fashioned, semicircular bow windows run from basement to roof of Roe Head; and look down upon a long green slope of pasture-land, ending in the pleasant woods of Kirklees, Sir George Armitage's Park. Although Roe Head and Haworth are not twenty miles apart, the aspect of the country is totally dissimilar as if they enjoyed a different climate. The soft curving and heaving landscape around the former gives a stranger the idea of cheerful airiness on the heights, and of sunny warmth in the broad green valleys below. It is just such a neighbourhood as the monks loved, and traces of the old Plantagenet times are to be met with everywhere, side by side with the manufacturing interests of the West Riding of today [meaning the late 1850s].

Here, the park of Kirklees, full of sunny glades, speckled with black shadows of immemorial yew trees; the grey pile of building, formerly a 'House of professed Ladies' [nuns of the Benedictine Order] – the mouldering stone in the depth of the wood, under which Robin Hood is said to lie; close outside the Park, an old stone-gabled house now a roadside inn, but which bears the name of the 'Three Nuns', and has a pictured sign to correspond. This quaint old inn is frequented by fustian-dressed* mill-hands from the neighbouring worsted factories, which strew the high road from Leeds to Huddersfield, and form the centre round which future villages gather.

Such are the contrasts of modes of living, and of times and seasons, brought before the traveller on the great roads that traverse the West Riding. In no other part of England, I fancy, are the centuries brought into such close strange contact as in the district in which Roe Head is situated. Within a walk from Miss Wooler's house – lie the remains of Howley Hall, now the property of Lord Cardigan, but formerly belonging to a branch of the Saviles. Near to it is Lady Anne's Well; 'Lady Anne,' according to tradition, having been worried and eaten by wolves as she sat by the

---

* Fustian – a dense weatherproof and hardwearing fabric, dating back to the sixteenth century, originally made by Cudworths of Yorkshire.

well, to which the indigo dye factory people from Birstall and Batley woollen mills yet repair on Palm Sunday, when the waters possess remarkable medicinal efficacy; and it is still believed that they assume a strange variety of colours at six o'clock in the morning on that day.

All round the lands held by the farmer who lives in the remains of Howley Hall are stone houses of today, occupied by the people who are making their living and their fortunes by the woollen mills that encroach upon, and shoulder out the proprieters of the ancient halls. These are to be seen in every direction, picturesque, many-gabled, with heavy stone carvings of coats of arms for heraldic ornament; belonging to decayed families, from whose ancestral lands field after field has been shorn away, by the urgency of rich manufacturers pressing hard upon necessity.

A smoky atmosphere surrounds these old dwellings of former Yorkshire squires, and blights and blackens the ancient trees that overshadow them; cinder paths lead up to them; the ground round about is sold for building upon; but still the neighbours, though they subsist by a different state of things remember that their forefathers lived in agricultural dependence upon the owners of these halls; and treasure up the traditions connected with the stately households that existed centuries ago. Take Oakwell Hall, for instance. It stands in a rough looking pasture-field, about a quarter of a mile from the high road. It is but that distance from the busy whirr of the steam-engines employed in the woollen mills of Birstall; and if you walk to it from Birstall Station about meal-time, you encounter strings of mill-hands, blue with woollen dye, and crunching in hungry haste over the cinder paths bordering the high road. Turning off from this to the right, you ascend through an old pasture-field, and enter a short by-road, called the

The Legend

'Bloody Lane' – a walk haunted by the ghost of a certain Captain Batt, the reprobate proprieter of an old hall close by, in the days of the Stuarts. From the 'Bloody Lane', overshadowed by trees, you come into the rough looking meadow in which Oakwell Hall is situated. It is known in the neighbourhood to be the place described as, 'Field Head', Shirley's residence. The enclosure in front, half court, half garden; the panelled hall, with the gallery opening into the bed-chambers, running round; the barbarous peach-coloured drawing-room; the bright lookout through the garden door upon the grassy lawns and terraces behind, where the soft-hued pigeons still love to coo and strut in the sun, – are described in Shirley. The scenery of that fiction lies close around; the real events which suggested it took place in the immediate neighbourhood.

They show a bloody footprint in a bedchamber of Oakwell Hall, and tell a story connected with it, and with the lane by which the house is approached. Captain Batt was believed to be far away; his family were at Oakwell; when in the dusk, one winter evening, he came stalking along the lane, and through the hall, and up the stairs, into his own room, where he vanished. He had been killed in a duel in London that very same afternoon of December 9, 1684.

The stones of the Hall formed part of the more ancient vicarage, which an ancestor of Captain Batt's had seized in the troublous times for property which succeeded the Reformation. This Henry Batt possessed himself of houses and money without scruple; and, at last, stole the great bell of Birstall Church, for which sacrilegious theft, a fine was imposed on the land, and has to be paid by the owner of the Hall to this day.

But the possession of the Oakwell property passed out of the hands of the Batts at the beginning of the last century;

collateral descendants succeeded, and left this picturesque trace of their having been. In the great hall hangs a mighty pair of stag's horns, and dependant from them, a printed card, recording the fact that, on the 1st September 1763, there was a great hunting match, when this stag was slain; and that fourteen gentlemen shared the chase, and dined on the spoil in that hall, along with Fairfax Fearnley esq., the owner. The fourteen names are given, doubtless, 'mighty men of yore'; but, among them all, Sir Fletcher Norton, Attorney-General, and Major-General Birch were the only ones with which I had any association in 1855.

Passing on from Oakwell, there lie houses right and left, which were well known to Miss Brontë when she lived at Roe Head, as the hospitable homes of some of her schoolfellows...

The number of pupils ranged from seven to ten, during the two years Miss Brontë was there; and as they did not require the whole of the house for their accommodation, the third storey was unoccupied, except by the ghostly idea of a lady clad in a rustling silk gown which was sometimes heard by the listeners at the foot of the second flight of stairs.

The Holly Tree

ROBERT SOUTHEY

Though somewhat condescending in his reply to Charlotte Brontë's first letter to him, the poet laureate was to come to respect her work before he died. The following poem, written in 1798, is considered his most famous.

O Reader! Hast thou ever stood to see the holly tree?
The eye that contemplates it well perceives
Its glossy leaves,
Ordered by an intelligence so wise,
As might confound the atheist's sophistries.

Below, a circling fence, its leaves are seen,
Wrinkled and keen;
No grazing cattle, through their prickly round,
Can reach a wound;
But as they grow where nothing is to fear,
Smooth and unarmed the pointless leaves appear.

I love to view these things with curious eyes,
And moralize:
And in this wisdom of the holly tree
Can emblems see,

Wherewith, perchance, to make a pleasant ryme,
One which may profit in the after time.

Thus, though abroad perchance I might appear
Harsh and austere,
To those who on my leisure would intrude
Reserved and rude,
Gentle at home amid my friends I'd be,
Like the high leaves upon the holly tree.

And should my youth, as youth is apt, I know,
Some harshness show,
All vain asperities day by day
Would wear away.
Till the smooth temper of my age should be
Like the high leaves upon the holly tree.

And as when all the summer trees are seen
So bright and green,
The holly leaves a sombre hue display,
Less bright than they;
But when the bare and wintry woods we see,
What then so cheerful as the holly tree?

So serious should my youth appear among
The thoughtless throng,
So would I seem among the young and gay
More grave than they,
That in my age as cheerful I might be
As the green winter of the holly tree.

Christmas Correspondence with the Poets

Christmas 1836 found the Brontës thinking of ways to create an income, so that they would not be so burdensome on their father's small stipend. As they all had some talent in writing, they decided that they should write to various literary figures to get their opinions. Charlotte began the process by writing to Robert Southey, the poet laureate; then Branwell wrote to Wordsworth, and to *Blackwood's Magazine*. As is common with many literary geniuses whose work later becomes popular, their initial attempts brought them little comfort, as the following extracts, taken from the letters collected by Shorter, Robert Southey's correspondence and Gaskell's biography, show.

The conversational and descriptive reply was admirable from so eminent a character, but rambled on at very great length!

Keswick, March 1837
Madam,

You will probably ere this, have given up all expectation of receiving an answer to your letter of December 29. I was on the borders of Cornwall when the letter was written; it found me a fortnight after in Hampshire. During my subsequent movements in different parts of the country, and a tarriance of three busy weeks in

London, I had no leisure for replying to it; and now I am once more at home, and am clearing off the arrears of business which have accumulated during a long absence, it has lain unanswered till the last of a numerous file, not from disrespect or indifference to its contents, but because, in truth, it is not an easy task to answer it, nor a pleasant one to cast a damp over the high spirits and generous desires of youth.

What you are I can only infer from your letter, which appears to be written in sincerity, though I may suspect you have used a fictitious signature. Be that as it may, the letter and verses bear the same stamp; and I can well understand the state of mind they indicate. What I am you may have learnt from such of my publications as have come into your hands; and had you happened to be acquainted with me, a little personal knowledge would have tempered your enthusiasm. You might have had your ardour in some degree abated by seeing a poet in the decline of life, and witnessing the effect that life has on our hopes and aspirations; yet I am neither a disappointed man nor a discontented one, and you would never have heard from me any chilling sermons upon the text, 'All is vanity'.

It is not my advice that you have asked as to the direction of your talents, but my opinion of them; and yet the opinion may be worth little, and the advice much. You evidently possess, and in no inconsiderable degree, what Wordsworth calls the 'faculty of verse'. I am not depreciating it when I say in these times it is not rare. Many volumes of poems are now published every year without attracting attention, any one of which, if it had appeared half a century ago, would have obtained a high reputation for its author.

Whoever, therefore, is ambitious of distinction in this way ought to be prepared for disappointment.

After a lengthy discourse upon the 'business of a woman's life,' Southey concludes thus:

But do not suppose I disparage the gift which you possess, nor that I would discourage you from exercising it. I only exhort you to think of it, and so to use it, as to render it conducive to your own permanent good. Write poetry for its own sake; not in a spirit of emulation, and not with a view to celebrity; the less you aim at the more likely you will be to deserve and finally obtain it . . .

Farewell, madam. It is not because I have forgotten that I was once young myself, that I write to you in this strain; but because I remember it. You will neither doubt my sincerity, nor my goodwill; and however ill what has here been said may accord with your present views and temper, the longer you live the more reasonable it will appear to you. Though I may be an ungracious adviser, you will allow me, therefore, to subscribe myself, with the best wishes for your happiness, here and hereafter,

your true friend,
Robert Southey

On the original of this letter is written, in Charlotte Brontë's handwriting, 'Southey's advice to be kept forever.'

Charlotte wrote back to Southey to thank him for his advice which she assured him would not be wasted, and to gently admonish him for assuming she used a false name. 'That letter is consecrated . . . If I live to be an old woman,

I shall remember it thirty years hence as a bright dream. The signature which you suspected of being fictitious is my real name. Again, therefore, I must sign myself, Charlotte Brontë.'

During the same holidays, Branwell sent the following letter and Christmas poem to William Wordsworth for similar appraisal:

January 19th 1837
Sir,

– I most earnestly entreat you to read and pass your judgement upon what I have sent you, because from the day of my birth to this the nineteenth year of my life, I have lived among secluded hills, where I could neither know what I was nor what I could do. I read for the same reason that I ate or drank; because it was a real craving of nature. I wrote on the same principle as I spoke – out of the impulse and feeling of the mind; nor could I help it, for what came out, came out, and there was the end of it. For as to self conceit, that could not receive food from flattery, since to this hour, not half a dozen people in the world know I have ever penned a line ...

Do pardon me, sir, that I have ventured to come before one whose works I have most loved in our literature, and who most has been with me a divinity of the mind, – laying before him one of my writings, and asking of him a judgement of its contents. I must come before some one from whose sentence there is no appeal; and such a one is he who has developed the theory of poetry as well as its practice, and both in such a way as to claim a place in the memory of a thousand years to come ...

Christmas Correspondence with the Poets

Now to send you the whole of this would be a mock upon your patience; what you see does not even pretend to be more than the description of an imaginative child. But read it, sir; and, as you would hold a light to one in utter darkness – as you value your own kindheartedness – return me an answer, if but one word, telling me whether I should write on, or write no more. Forgive undue warmth, because my feelings in this matter cannot be cool; and believe me sir, with deep respect,

your really humble servant,
P.B. Brontë

So where he reigns in glory bright,
Above those starry skies of night,
Amid his paradise of light
Oh, why may I not be?

Oft when awake on Christmas morn,
In sleepless twilight laid forlorn,
Strange thoughts have o'er my mind been borne,
How He died for me.

And oft within my chamber lying
Have I awaked myself with crying
from dreams, where I beheld Him dying
Upon the accursed Tree.

And oft has my mother said,
While on her lap I laid my head,
She feared for time I was not made,
But for Eternity.

So, 'I can read my title clear,
To mansions in the skies
And let me bid farewell to fear,
And wipe my weeping eyes.'

I'll lay me down on this marble stone.
And set the world aside,
To see upon her ebon throne
The Moon in glory ride.

    Did Wordsworth answer Branwell's letter? I am not sure. However, the comment appears in Mrs Gaskell:

It [the letter] was given by the poet to Mr Quillian in 1850, after the name of Brontë had become known and famous. I have no means of ascertaining what answer was returned by Mr Wordsworth; but that he considered the letter remarkable may, I think, be inferred both from its preservation, and its recurrence to his memory when the real name of Currer Bell was made known to the public.

Music on a Christmas Morn

ACTON BELL

One of Anne Brontë's poems, written under her pseudonym: this is the only truly Christmas poem written by any of the Brontës. The original was first published in 1849, and again by Smith, Elder and Co. in the *Life and Works of Charlotte Brontë and Her Sisters*, in 1899, whence this copy is taken.

This was probably written by Anne during one of her Christmas holidays which she always spent at home. The bells she refers to cannot have been those of her own church though, as the bells of Haworth Church, a peal of six, were bought by public subscription, cast in 1845 and rung for the first time in March 1846. The poem was first published in a volume of the sisters' poems which was published in May of that year.

Anne uses many phrases from traditional Christmas carols in this poem, as well as references from them in her own lines. The influence of 'Christians Awake', a most popular carol at the time, is clear in the second and third verses, and she draws from 'While Shepherds Watched' in the fourth. Put to music, it would have made a strong companion to these famous Christmas hymns, given the chance.

Music I love – but never strain
Could kindle raptures so divine,
So grief assuage, so conquer pain,
And rouse this pensive heart of mine –
As that we hear on Christmas Morn
Upon the wintry breezes borne.

Though Darkness still her empire keep,
And hours must pass, ere morning break
From troubled dreams or slumbers deep,
That music kindly bids us wake:
It calls us with an angel's voice,
To wake, and worship, and rejoice.
To greet with joy the glorious morn,
Which angels welcomed long ago,
When our redeeming Lord was born,
To bring the light of Heaven below;
The Powers of Darkness to dispel,
And rescue Earth from Death and Hell.

While listening to that sacred strain,
My raptured spirit soars on high;
I seem to hear those songs again
Resounding through the open sky,
That kindled such divine delight
In those who watched their flocks by night.

Music on a Christmas Morn

With them I celebrate his birth –
Glory to God in the Highest Heaven,
Goodwill to men, and peace on earth,
To us a Saviour-king is given,
Our God is come to claim his own,
And Satan's power is overthrown.

A sinless God, for sinful men,
Descends to suffer and to bleed;
Hell must renounce its empire then;
The price is paid, the world is freed,
And Satan's self must now confess
That Christ has earned a Right to bless:

Now holy peace may smile from Heaven,
And heavenly Truth from earth shall spring;
The captive's galling bonds are riven,
For our Redeemer is our King;
And He that gave His blood for men
Will lead us home to God again.

Tabby's Icy Accident

Another extract from Mrs Gaskell's *Life of Charlotte Brontë*.

The Christmas holidays came, and she [Charlotte] and Anne returned to the parsonage and to that happy home circle in which alone their natures expanded; amongst all other people they shrivelled up more or less. Indeed, there were only one or two strangers who could be admitted among the sisters without producing the same result. Emily and Anne were bound up in their lives and interests like twins. The former from reserve, the latter from timidity, avoided all friendships and intimacies beyond their sisters. Emily was impervious to influence; she never came into contact with public opinion, and her own view on what was right and fitting was a law for her conduct and appearance, with which she allowed no-one to interfere. Her love was poured out on Anne, as Charlotte's was on her. But the affection among the three was stronger than either life or death.

E. [Ellen Nussey] was eagerly welcomed by Charlotte, freely admitted by Emily and kindly received by Anne, whenever she could come amongst them; and this Christmas she had promised to visit Haworth, but her coming had to be delayed on account of a little domestic accident detailed in the following letter:

Tabby's Icy Accident

Dec. 29th 1837
I am sure you will have thought me very remiss, in not sending my promised letter long before now; but I have a sufficient and very melancholy excuse in an accident that befell our faithful old Tabby, a few days after my return home. She was gone out into the village on some errand, when, as she was descending the steep street, her foot slipped on the ice, and she fell; it was dark, and no-one saw her mischance, till after a time her groans attracted the attention of a passer-by. She was lifted up and carried into the Druggist's near; and, after the examination, it was discovered that she had completely shattered and dislocated one leg. Unfortunately the fracture could not be set until six o'clock the next morning, as no surgeon was to be had before that time, and she now lies at our house in a very doubtful and dangerous state. Of course, we are all extremely distressed at the circumstance, for she is like one of our own family. Since the event we have been almost without assistance – a person has dropped in now and then to do the drudgery, but we have, as yet, been able to procure no regular servant; and, consequently, the whole work of the house, as well as the additional duty of nursing Tabby, falls on ourselves. Under these circumstances, I dare not press your visit here, at least until she is pronounced out of danger; it would be too selfish of me. Aunt wished me to give you this information before, but papa and all the rest were anxious I should delay until we saw whether matters took a more settled aspect, and I myself kept putting it off from day to day, most bitterly reluctant to give up all the pleasure I had anticipated so long. However, remembering what you told me, namely, that you had commended the matter to a higher decision than ours, and that you were resolved to submit with resignation to that decision,

whatever it might be, I hold it my duty to yield also, and to be silent; it may be all for the best. I fear, if you had been here during this severe weather your visit would have been of no advantage to you, for the moors are blockaded with snow, and you would never have been able to get out. After this disappointment, I never dare reckon with certainty on the enjoyment of pleasure again; it seems as if some fatality stood between you and me ...

> After this event, and Tabby no longer in any danger, it was suggested by the prudent aunt that she should go to her sister's for nursing, thereby leaving the meagre resources of the parsonage in store for the rest of the Christmas holidays, as well as restoring the freedom and relaxed manner of the holidays upon the girls who otherwise were destined to spend the whole Christmas nursing. However, we are told by Mrs Gaskell that the girls were so incensed by this proposed treatment of their old nurse that they went on a hunger strike until the idea was rescinded, as she put it, 'The strong feeling of Duty being paramount to Pleasure'!
>
> Two years later it was evident that they had to accept the fact of life without Tabby, as Charlotte writes again to her friend Ellen Nussey:

December 21st. 1839

We are at present, and have been during the past month, rather busy, for that space of time we have been without a servant, except a little girl to run errands. Poor Tabby became so lame she was at length obliged to leave us. She is residing with her sister, in a little house of her own, which she bought with her savings a year or two since. She is very comfortable, and wants nothing, as she is near we see her very often.

In the meantime Emily and I have been sufficiently busy, as you may suppose: I manage the ironing, and keep the rooms clean; Emily does the baking, and attends to the kitchen. We are such odd animals, that we prefer this mode of contrivance to having a new face amongst us. Besides, we do not despair of Tabby's return, and she shall not be supplanted by a stranger in her absence. I excited aunt's wrath very much by burning the clothes the first time I attempted to iron; but I do better now. Human feelings are queer things; I am much happier blackleading the stoves, making the beds, and sweeping the floors at home, than I should be living like a fine lady anywhere else ... I intend to force myself to take another situation when I can get one, though I hate and abhor the idea of governess-ship. But I must do it, and therefore I heartily wish I could hear of a family where they need such a commodity as a governess.

In July 1842, the sisters found themselves in Brussels at M. Heger's school. There they perfected their French, lived a much more social life than ever at home, and yet still longed for the family hearth. So it was that they all gathered as always at Christmastide. Mrs Gaskell takes up the detail:

... They enjoyed their Christmas all together inexpressibly. Branwell was with them; that was always a pleasure at this time; whatever might be his faults, or even, his vices, his sisters yet held him up as their family hope, as they trusted that he would one day be their family pride. They blinded themselves to the magnitude of the failings of which they were now and then told, by persuading themselves that such failings were common to all men of any strength or character; for, till sad experience taught them better, they fell into the usual error of confounding strong passions with strong character.

Charlotte's friend came over to see her, and she returned the visit. Her Brussels life must have seemed like a dream, so completely, in this short space of time, did she fall back into the old household ways; and with more household independence than she could ever have had during her aunt's lifetime. Winter though it was, the sisters took their accustomed walks on the snowcovered moors; or went often down the road to Keighley, for such books as had been added to the library there during their long absence from England.

Church-Decking

WILLIAM WORDSWORTH

Wordsworth was a well-respected contemporary of the Brontës. This short poem touches on the custom of decorating the churches for Christmastide.

Would that our scrupulous sires had dared to leave
Less scanty measure of those graceful rites
And usages, who due return invites
A stir of mind too natural to deceive;
Giving the memory help when she could weave
A crown for Hope! – I dread the boasted lights
That all too often are but fiery blights,
Killing the bud o'er which in vain we grieve.

Go, seek when Christmas snows discomfort bring,
The counter spirit found in some gay church
Green with fresh holly, every pew a perch
In which the linnet or the thrush might sing,
Merry and loud, and safe from prying search,
Strains offered only to the genial spring.

The Sparkling Bough

WILLIAM MAKEPEACE THACKERAY

When he was not writing severe criticisms of all and sundry, Thackeray could be very Christmassy indeed! He wrote about children's parties, Christmas dinner, pantomime and Christmas trees, among other aspects of the festive season. The following is a delightful Christmas piece about the tree and its contents, bonbons (which were the forerunner of the Christmas cracker), and the usual spate of Christmas bills which do not seem to have changed all that much in the last 150 years!

The kindly Christmas Tree, from which I trust, every gentle reader has pulled a bonbon or two, is yet all aflame whilst I am writing, and sparkles with the sweet fruits of its season. You young ladies, may you have plucked pretty giftlings from it; and out of the cracker sugar-plum which you have split with the captain or the sweet young curate, may you have read one of those delicious conundrums which the confectioners introduce into the sweetmeats, and which apply to the cunning passion of Love. Those riddles are to be read at your age, when I dare say they were amusing. As for Dolly, Merry & Bell, who are standing at the tree, they don't care about the love-riddle part, but understand the sweet-almond part very well. They are four, five, six years old. Patience, little people! A dozen merry Christmasses more, a dozen merry Christmasses more and you will be reading those wonderful love-conundrums, too.

As for us elderly folk, we watch the babies at their sport, and the young people pulling at the branches: and instead of finding bonbons or sweeties in the packets which we pluck off the boughs, we find Mr Carnifax's review of the quarter's meat; Mr Sartor's compliments, and the statement for self and the young gentlemen; and Madame de Sainte-Crinoline's respects to the young ladies, who encloses her account, and will send on Saturday, please; or we stretch out our hand to the educational branch of the Christmas tree, and there find a lively and amusing article from the Reverend Henry Holyshade, containing our dear Tommy's exceedingly moderate account for the last term's school expenses.

Thackeray's Christmas Criticism

The mutual respect for each other's work grew between Charlotte Brontë and Thackeray over several years. Charlotte read much of his writings, and may well have found this item of interest. From *Fraser's Magazine*, February 1844, it is a literary criticism on their fellow contemporary Charles Dickens's *Christmas Carol*:

Who can listen to objections regarding such a book as this? It seems to me a national benefit, and to every man or woman who reads it a personal kindness. The last two people I heard speak of it were women; neither knew the other, or the author, and both said, by way of criticism, 'God bless him!' A Scotch philosopher, who nationally does not keep Christmas Day, on reading the book, sent out for a turkey, and asked two friends to dine, – this is fact! Many men were known to sit down, after perusing it, and write off letters to their friends, not about business, but out of their fulness of heart, and to wish old acquaintances a happy Christmas. Had the book appeared a fortnight earlier, all the prize cattle would have been gobbled up in pure love and friendship, Epping denuded of sausages, and not a turkey left in Norfolk. His royal highness's fatstock would have fetched unheard of prices, and Alderman Bannister would have tired of slaying....

As for Tiny Tim, there is a certain passage in the book regarding that young gentleman, about which a man should hardly venture to speak in print or in public, any more than he would of any other affections of his private heart. There is not a reader in England but that little creature will be a bond of union between the author and him; and he will say of Charles Dickens, as the woman said just now, 'God bless him!' What a feeling is this for a writer to be able to inspire, and what a reward to reap!

The Cheerful Hearth

EMILY BRONTË

This four-line verse by Emily Brontë was found written out in a neat longhand on a scrap of paper used as a bookmark in a book of verse found in a second-hand shop in Keighley by the author many years ago. An extract in the *Oxford Companion to English Literature* states: 'In 1845 she (Charlotte) discovered, (or so she alleged) the poems of Emily, and convinced of their quality, projected a joint publication; a volume of verse entitled, "Poems of Currer, Ellis & Acton Bell" [the pseudonyms of Charlotte, Emily and Anne] appeared in 1846, but did not sell and received little attention.'

The manuscript poem in the author's possession is certainly of the nineteenth century, but probably copied out of that original publication by a reader, rather than by Emily herself!

Cheerful is the hearth, soft the matted floor,
Not one shivering gust creeps through pane or door,
The little lamp burns straight, its rays shoot strong and far,
I trim it well, to be the wanderer's guiding star.

Juvenile Parties – A Remonstrance Concerning Them

WILLIAM MAKEPEACE THACKERAY

The most popular custom of a children's party early in the evening before the adults' party began was a practical as well as pleasurable event for all concerned during the eighteenth and nineteenth centuries. The idea originally was that families could all attend, with the children being catered for first then packed off to bed or taken home by nurses, while their parents continued long into the night. This event usually coincided with the Twelfth Night Fancy Dress Ball. In the nineteenth century, the old festival of Holy Innocents, 28 December, was revived as a day for children. By having the children's party on this day, the number of possibilities for a party became Christmas, Innocents, New Year and Twelfth Night!

For the purpose of the item reproduced here from 'The Snobs of England', published at Christmas 1846, Mr Thackeray takes on the personage of a harassed gentleman of some substance with a large, socially acceptable family. He is writing to the editor of *Punch* magazine accusing him of further popularising the party custom. The piece is entitled 'Juvenile Parties – A Remonstrance Concerning Them'. Things simply do not change! Hands up all those who know exactly what Mr Thackeray is talking about!

THE PARTY ...

The awful spread of Juvenile parties, sir, is the fact to which I would draw your attention. There is no end to those entertainments, and if the custom be not speedily checked, people will be obliged to fly from London at Christmas and hide their children during the holidays. I gave mine warning in a speech at breakfast this day, and said with tears in my eyes that if the Juvenile Party system went on, I would take a house at Margate next winter, for that, by heavens! I could not bear another Juvenile Season in London.

If they would but transfer Innocents Day to the summer holidays, and let the children have their pleasures in May or June, we might get on. But now, in this most ruthless and cutthroat season of sleet, thaw, frost, wind, snow, mud and sore throats, it is a quite tempting fate to be going much abroad, and this is the time of all others that is selected for the amusement of our little darlings.

... You, sir, have by your agents, caused not a little of the mischief. I desire that, during Christmas time at least, Mr Leech shall be abolished, or sent to take a holiday. Judging from his sketches, I should say that he must be endowed with a perfectly monstrous organ of philoprogenitiveness; he revels in the delineation of the dearest and most beautiful little boys and girls in turn-down collars and broad sashes, and produces in your Almanack a picture of a child's costume ball, in which he has made the little wretches in the dresses of every age, and looking so happy, beautiful and charming, that I have carefully kept the picture from the women and children of my household, and – I will not say burned it, for I have not the heart to do that – but locked it away privately, lest they should conspire to have a costume ball themselves, and little Polly should insist on appearing in the address of Anne Boleyn, or little Jacky upon turning out as an Ancient Briton.

... The real satirist has no right to lead the public astray about the Juvenile Fete nuisance, and to describe a Ball as if it were some sort of Paradise and all the little imps engaged as happy and pretty as so many cherubs, when in fact they should be drawn as hideous – disagreeable – distorted – affected – jealous of each other – dancing awkwardly – with shoes too tight for them – overeating themselves at supper – very unwell (and deservedly so) the next morning, with Mamma administering a mixture after the Doctor's prescription, and which shall be painted awfully black, in an immense large teacup, and (as might be shown by the horrible expression on the little patient's face) of the most disgusting flavour!

THE INCONVENIENCE ...
... I am the deplorable chaperone of the young people. I am called upon to conduct my young family five miles to tea at six o'clock. No count is taken of our personal habits, hours of dinner, or intervals of rest. We are made the victims of an infantile conspiracy, nor will the lady of the house hear of any revolt or denial.

'Why', says she, with the spirit which becomes a woman and a mother, 'you go to your man's parties eagerly enough: what an un-natural wretch you must be to grudge your children their pleasures!' She looks round, sweeps all six of them into her arms, whilst the baby in her lap begins to bawl, and you are assailed by seven pairs of imploring eyes, against which there is no appeal. You must go. If you are dying of lumbago, if you are engaged in the best of dinners, if you are longing to stop at home and read McCaulay, you must give up all and go.

And it is not to be one party or two, but to almost all. You must go to Gravel Pits, otherwise the grandmother will cut the children out of her will and leave everything to the other grandchildren. If you refuse Islington and accept Tyburn Gardens, you sneer at a poor relation, and acknowledge a rich one readily enough. If you decline Tyburn Gardens, you fling away the chances of the poor, dear children in life, and the hopes of cadetship for little Jacky. If you go to Hampstead, having declined Bedford Place, it is because you never refuse an invitation to Hampstead, where they make much of you, and Miss Maria is pretty, (as you think, though your wife doesn't) and do not care for the Doctor in Bedford Place. And if you accept Bedford Place you dare not refuse Upper Baker Street, because there is a coolness between the two families, and you must on no account seem to take part with one or the other.

THE EXPENSE...

... The expenses of children's toiletries at this present time are perfectly frightful.

My eldest boy, Gustavus, at home from Dr Birch's Academy... wears turquoise studs, fine linen shirts, white waistcoats, and shiny boots; yet, when I proposed he should go to a party in Berlin gloves, asked me if I wished he should be mistaken for a footman! My second son, Augustus, grumbles about getting his elder brother's clothes, nor could he be brought to accommodate himself to Gustavus's waistcoats at all, had his mother not coaxed him by the loan of her chain and watch, which latter the child broke after many desperate attempts to wind it up. As for the little

Juvenile Parties – A Remonstrance Concerning Them

fellow, Adolphus, his mother has him attired in a costume partly Scotch, partly Hungarian, mostly buttons, and with a Louis Quatorze hat and scarlet feather, and she curls this child's hair with her own blessed tongs every night.

I wish she would do as much for the girls, though: but no, Monsieur Floridor must do that: and accordingly, every day this season, that abominable little Frenchman comes over, and at a cost of eighteen pence par tête, figs out my little creatures' heads with fixative, bandoline, crinoline – the deuce knows what.

The bill for silk stockings, sashes, white frocks, is so enormous, that I have not been able to pay my own tailor for three years.

. . . Having to go to Hackney in the snow, on the night of the 5th January, our man was so hopelessly inebriated, that I was compelled to get out and drive myself; and I am now, on what is called Twelfth Day (with of course, another children's party before me for the evening) writing this from my bed, sir, with a severe cold, a violent toothache, and a most acute rheumatism.

Christmas at Wuthering Heights

EMILY BRONTË

A seasonal extract from Emily's tale, *Wuthering Heights*, which takes place at the house of that name. His former champion, old Mr Earnshaw, having died, the young Heathcliff is a neglected soul and wild. His only playmate is Catherine Earnshaw with whom he has been told he must not speak. She is sent away to Thrushcross Grange to recover from a broken ankle, and learn some manners at the hand of the polite Mrs Linton. We take up the story just before Christmas, and Cathy is come home. She has emerged from a wild little thing to a dignified young lady. Meanwhile, Heathcliff has been even more alone and neglected save for the attentions of the servant, Nelly.

The wide contrast between the two distinct types of Yorkshire Christmas is apparent between the cosy traditionalist, Nelly, and her fellow servant, Joseph, who abhors everything to do with the festival.

Cathy stayed at Thrushcross Grange five weeks, till Christmas. By that time her ankle was thoroughly cured, and her manners much improved. The mistress visited her often in the interval, and commenced her plan of reform by trying to raise her self-respect with fine

Christmas at Wuthering Heights

clothes and flattery, which she took readily; so that, instead of a wild hatless little savage jumping into the house, and rushing to squeeze us all breathless, there alighted from a handsome black pony a very dignified person with brown ringlets falling from the cover of a feathered beaver, and a long cloth habit, which she was obliged to hold up with both hands that she might sail in....

She kissed me gently; I was in flour, making the Christmas Cake, and it would not have done to give me a hug; and then she looked around for Heathcliff. Mr and Mrs Earnshaw watched anxiously their meeting, thinking it would enable them to judge, in some measure, what grounds they had for hoping to succeed in separating the two friends.

Heathcliff was hard to discover at first. If he were careless and uncared for before Catherine's absence, he had been ten times more so since.

Nobody but I even did him the courtesy of calling him a dirty boy, and bid him wash himself once a week; and children of his age seldom have a natural pleasure in soap and water. Therefore, not to mention his clothes, which had seen three months' service in mire and dust, and his thick uncombed hair, the surface of his face and hands were dismally beclouded. He might well skulk behind the settle, on beholding such a bright graceful damsel enter the house, instead of a rough headed counterpart of himself, as he expected.

'Is Heathcliff not here?' she demanded, pulling off her gloves, and displaying fingers whitened with doing nothing and staying indoors.

'Heathcliff, you may come forward,' cried Mr Hindley, enjoying his discomfiture, and gratified to see what a forbidding young blackguard he would be compelled to present himself. 'You may come and wish Catherine welcome, like all the other servants.'

Cathy, catching a glimpse of her friend in his concealment, flew to embrace him; she bestowed seven or eight kisses on his cheek within the second, and then stopped, and drawing back, burst into a laugh, exclaiming

'Why, how very black and cross you look! and how – how funny and grim! But that's because I'm used to Edgar and Isabella Linton. Well, Heathcliff, have you forgotten me?'

She had some reason to put the question, for shame and pride threw double gloom over his countenance, and kept him immovable....

After playing lady's maid to the newcomer, and putting my cakes in the oven, and making the house and kitchen cheerful with great fires, befitting Christmas Eve, I prepared to sit down and amuse myself by singing carols all alone; regardless of Joseph's affirmations that he considered the merry tunes I chose as next door to songs.

He had retired to pray in his chamber, and Mr and Mrs Earnshaw were engaging Missy's attention by sundry gay trifles bought for her to present to the little Lintons, as an acknowledgement for their kindness.

They had invited them to spend the morrow at Wuthering Heights, and the invitation had been accepted, on one condition; Mrs Linton begged that her darlings might be kept carefully apart from that 'naughty, swearing boy'.

Under these circumstances I remained solitary. I smelt the rich scent of the heating spices; and admired the shining kitchen utensils, the polished clock decked with holly, the silver mugs ranged on a tray ready to be filled with mulled ale for supper, and above all, the speckless purity of my particular care – the scoured and well swept floor.

I gave due inward applause to every object, and I remembered how old Earnshaw used to come in when all was tidied, and call me a cant lass, and slip a shilling into my hand as a Christmas-box; and from that I went on to think of his fondness for Heathcliff, and his dread lest he should suffer neglect after death had removed him; and this naturally led me to consider the poor lad's situation now, and from singing I changed my mind to crying. It struck me soon, however, there would be more sense in endeavouring to repair some of his wrongs than shedding tears over them. I got up and walked into the court to seek him. He was not far; I found him smoothing the glossy coat of the new pony in the stable, and feeding the other beasts according to custom.

'Make haste, Heathcliff!' I said. 'The kitchen is so comfortable, and Joseph is upstairs; make haste and let me dress you smart before Miss Cathy comes out, and then you can sit together, with the whole hearth to yourselves, and have a long chatter till bed-time.'

He proceeded with his task, and never turned his head towards me.

'Come – Are you coming?' I continued. 'There's a little cake for each of you, nearly enough; and you'll need half-an-hour's donning.'

I waited five minutes, but getting no answer left him. Catherine supped with her brother and sister-in-law; Joseph and I joined at an unsocial meal, seasoned with reproofs on one side and sauciness on the other. His cake and cheese remained on the table all night for the fairies. He managed to continue work until nine o'clock, and then marched dumb and dour to his chamber.

Cathy sat up late, having a world of things to order for the reception of her new friends; she came into the kitchen once more to speak to her old one; but he was gone, and she only stayed to ask what was the matter with him, and then went back.

In the morning he rose early; and as it was a holiday, carried his ill humour onto the moors, not re-appearing till the family were departed for church. Fasting and reflection seem to have brought him to a better spirit. He hung about me for a while, and having screwed up his courage, exclaimed abruptly, –

'Nelly, make me decent; I'm going to be good.'

... I chattered on, and Heathcliff gradually lost his frown and began to look quite pleasant, when all at once our conversation was interrupted by a rumbling sound moving up the road and entering the court. He ran to the window and I to the door just in time to see the two Lintons descend from the family carriage, smothered in cloaks and furs, and the Earnshaws dismount from their horses; they often rode to church in winter. Catherine took a hand of each of the children, and brought them into the house and set them before the fire, which quickly put colour into their white faces.

I urged my companion to hasten now and show his amiable humour, and he willingly obeyed; but ill-luck would have it that, as he opened the door leading from the kitchen on one side, Hindley opened it on the other. They met, and the Master, irritated at seeing him clean and cheerful – or, perhaps, eager to keep his promise to Mrs Linton, shoved him back with a sudden thrust, and angrily bade Joseph, 'Keep the fellow out of the room; send him into the garret till dinner is over. He'll be cramming his fingers in the tarts and stealing the fruit, if left alone with them a minute.'

'Nay sir,' I could not avoid answering, 'he'll touch nothing, not he; and I suppose he must have his share of the dainties as well as we.'

'He shall have his share of my hand if I catch him downstairs till dark!' cried Hindley. 'Begone, you vagabond! What! you are attempting the coxcomb are you, wait till I get hold of those elegant locks – see if I won't pull them a bit longer!'

'They are long enough already,' observed Mister Linton, peeping from the doorway; 'I wonder they don't make his head ache. It's like a colt's mane over his eyes!'

He ventured this remark without any intention to insult; but Heathcliff's violent nature was not prepared to endure the appearance of impertinence from one whom he seemed to hate, even then, as a rival. He seized a tureen of hot apple sauce, the first thing that came under his grip, and dashed it full against the speaker's face and neck, who instantly commenced a lament that brought Isabella and Catherine hurrying to the place.

Mr Earnshaw snatched up the culprit directly and conveyed him to his chamber; where, doubtless, he administered a rough remedy to cool the fit of passion....

'There, there, children, to your seats!' cried Hindley, bustling in, 'That brute of a lad has warmed me nicely. Next time, Master Edgar, take the law into your own fists – it will give you an appetite!'

The little party recovered its equanimity at sight of the fragrant feast. They were hungry after their ride, and easily consoled, since no real harm had befallen them.

Mr Earnshaw carved bountiful platefuls and the mistress made them merry with lively talk. I waited behind her chair, and was pained to behold Catherine, with dry eyes and an indifferent air, commence cutting up the wing of a goose before her.

'An unfeeling child,' I thought to myself; 'how lightly she dismisses her old playmate's troubles. I could not have imagined her to be so selfish.'

She lifted a mouthful to her lips; then she set it down again: her cheeks flushed, and the tears gushed over them.

She slipped her fork to the floor, and hastily dived under the cloth to conceal her emotion. I did not call her unfeeling long: for I perceived she was in purgatory throughout the day, and wearying to find an opportunity of getting by herself, or paying a visit to Heathcliff, who had been locked up by the Master, as I discovered, on endeavouring to introduce him to a private mess of victuals.

In the evening we had a dance. Cathy begged that he might be liberated then, as Isabella Linton had no partner; her entreaties were vain, and I was appointed to supply the deficiency.

We got rid of all the gloom in the excitement of the exercise, and our pleasure was increased by the arrival of the Gimmerton band, mustering fifteen strong – a trumpet, a trombone, clarionets, basoons, French horns, and a bass viol, besides singers. They go the round of all the respectable houses, and receive contributions every Christmas, and we esteemed it a first rate treat to hear them.

After the usual carols had been sung, we set them to songs and glees. Mrs Earnshaw loved the music and so they gave us plenty.

Catherine loved it too, but she said it sounded sweetest at the top of the steps, and she went up in the dark. I followed. They shut the house door below, never noting our absence; it was so full of people. She made no stay at the stairs' head, but mounted farther, to the garret where Heathcliff was confined, and called him...

I let the poor things converse unmolested, till I supposed the songs were going to cease, and the singers to get some refreshment; then I clambered up the ladder to warn her.

Instead of finding her outside, I heard her voice within. The little monkey had crept by the skylight of one garret, along the roof, into the skylight of the other, and it was with the utmost difficulty I could coax her out again. When she did come, Heathcliff came with her, and she insisted I should take him into the kitchen, as my fellow servant had gone to a neighbour's to be removed from the sound of our 'devil's psalmody', as it pleased him to call it.

I told them I intended by no means to encourage their tricks; but as the prisoner had never broken his fast since yesterday's dinner, I would wink at his cheating Mr Hindley that once.

December

PATRICK BRANWELL BRONTË

The desolate earth, the wintry sky,
The ceaseless rain-showers driving by –
The farewell of the year –
Though drear the sight, and sad the sound,
While bitter winds are wailing round,
Nor hopes depress, nor thoughts confound,
Nor waken sigh or tear.

For, as it moans, December's wind
Brings many varied thoughts to mind
Upon its storm-drenched wing,
Of words, not said 'mid sunshine gay,
Of deeds, not done in summer's day,
Yet which, when joy has passed away,
Will strength to sorrow bring.

For when the leaves are glittering bright,
And green hills lie in noonday night,
The present only lives;
But when within my chimnies roar
The chidings of the stormy shower,

December

The feeble present loses power,
The mighty past survives.

I cannot think – as roses blow,
And streams sound gently in their flow,
And clouds shine bright above –
Of aught but childhood's happiness,
Of joys unshadowed by distress
Or voices tuned the ear to bless
Or faces made to love.

But, when these winter evenings fall
Like dying nature's funeral pall,
The Soul gains strength to say
That – not aghast at stormy skies –
That – not bowed down by miseries, –
Its thoughts have will and power to rise
Above the present day.

A Ball, a Game of Charades and Christmas Baking

AN EXTRACT FROM *JANE EYRE* BY CHARLOTTE BRONTË

In Charlotte's most famous novel about a young girl whose early life is as a despised dependant acquainted with misery until she comes into her own inheritance, the storyline is narrated by Jane Eyre herself. Several Christmases are passed by in a flurry of snowy words: 'November, December and January passed...'. A few others are recorded and described, first with a child's memory, then as a young woman, looking on, and later describing the glittering ball to a visitor:

'Are there ladies at the Leas?'

'There are Mrs Eshton and her three daughters, very elegant young ladies indeed; and there are the Hon. Blanche and Mary Ingram, most beautiful women, I suppose: Indeed, I have seen Blanche, six or seven years since, when she was a girl of eighteen. She came here to a Christmas Ball and party Mr Rochester gave. You should have seen the dining room that day – how richly it was decorated, how brilliantly lit up! I should think there were fifty ladies and

A Ball, a Game of Charades and Christmas Baking

gentlemen present – all of the first county families: and Miss Ingram was considered the belle of the evening...'

The dining room doors were thrown open, and, as it was Christmas-time, the servants were allowed to assemble in the hall, to hear some of the ladies sing and play. Mr Rochester would have me come in, and I sat down in a quiet corner and watched them. I never saw a more splendid scene; the ladies were magnificently dressed; most of them – at least most of the younger ones – looked handsome; but Miss Ingram was certainly the queen....

> The most expansive is the description of the charades played by Mr Rochester and his party. Charades were very much a traditional Christmas pastime, and Miss Brontë does not actually say in her narrative whether this occasion took place at Christmas or not, as the preceding description is of life in general at Thornfield Hall, so it could even be a rainy spring evening. However, as the game is more usually associated with Christmas, and the description possibly the most vivid contemporary account of the game and its bustling preparation, it seems appropriate to reproduce the text here:

Merry were these days at Thornfield Hall; and busy days too: how different from the first three months of stillness, monotony, and solitude I had passed beneath its roof! All sad feelings seemed now driven from the house, all gloomy associations forgotten: there was life everywhere, movement all day long. You could not now traverse the gallery, once so hushed, nor enter the front chambers, once so tenantless, without encountering a smart lady's maid or a dandy valet.

The kitchen, the butler's pantry, the servants' hall, the entrance hall, were equally alive; and the saloons were only left void and still when the blue sky and halcyon sunshine of the genial spring weather called their occupants out into the grounds. Even when the weather was broken, and continuous rain set in for days, no damp seemed cast over enjoyment: indoor amusements only became more lively and varied, in consequence of the stop put to outdoor gaiety.

I wondered what they were going to do the first evening a change of entertainment was proposed: they spoke of 'playing Charades' but in my ignorance I did not understand the term. The servants were called in, the dining room tables wheeled away, the lights otherwise disposed, the chairs placed in a semicircle opposite the arch. While Mr Rochester and the other gentlemen directed these alterations, the ladies were running up and down stairs, ringing for their maids. Mrs Fairfax was summoned to give information respecting the resources of the house in shawls, dresses, draperies of any kind; and certain wardrobes of the third storey were ransacked, and their contents in the shape of brocaded and hooped petticoats, satin saques, black modes, lace lappets &c., were brought down in armfuls by the abigails; then a selection was made, and such things as were chosen were carried to the boudoir within the drawing room.

Meanwhile, Mr Rochester had again summoned the ladies round him, and was selecting certain of their number to be of his party. 'Miss Ingram is mine, of course,' said he: afterwards he named the two Misses Eshton and Mrs Dent. He looked at me: I happened to be near him, as I had been fastening the clasp of Mrs Dent's bracelet, which had got loose.

'Will you play?' he asked. I shook my head. He did not insist, which I rather feared he would have done; he allowed me to return quietly to my usual seat.

A Ball, a Game of Charades and Christmas Baking

He and his aids now withdrew behind the curtains: the other party, which was headed by Colonel Dent, sat down on the crescent of chairs. One of the gentlemen, Mr Eshton, observing me, seemed to propose that I should be asked to join them; but Lady Ingram instantly negatived the notion.

'No,' I heard her say, 'she looks too stupid for any game of the sort.'

Ere long a bell tinkled and the curtain drew up. Within the arch, the bulky figure of Sir George Lynn, whom Mr Rochester had likewise chosen, was seen enveloped in a white sheet: before him, on the table, lay a large book; and at his side stood Amy Eshton, draped in Mr Rochester's cloak, and holding a book in her hand. Somebody, unseen, rang the bell merrily; then Adele (who had insisted on being one of her guardian's party) bounded forward, scattering round her the contents of a basket of flowers she carried on her arm. Then appeared the magnificent figure of Miss Ingram, clad in white, a long veil on her head, and a wreath of roses round her brow; by her side walked Mr Rochester, and together they drew near the table. They knelt; while Mrs Dent and Louisa Eshton, dressed also in white, took up their stations behind them. A ceremony followed, in dumb show, in which it was easy to recognize the pantomime of a marriage. At its termination, Colonel Dent and his party consulted in whispers for two minutes, then the Colonel called out – 'Bride!' Mr Rochester bowed, and the curtain fell.

A considerable interval elapsed before it again rose. Its second rising displayed a more elaborately prepared scene than the last. The drawing room as I have before observed, was raised two steps above the dining room, and on the top of the upper step, placed a yard or two back within the room, appeared a large marble basin, which I recognised as an ornament from the conservatory – where it usually stood, surrounded by exotics, and tenanted by goldfish – whence it must have been transported with some trouble, on account of its size and weight.

Seated on the carpet by the side of this basin, was seen Mr Rochester, costumed in shawls, with a turban on his head. His dark eyes and swarthy skin and Paynim features suited the costume exactly: he looked the very model of an Eastern emir, and agent or a victim of the bow-string. Presently advanced into view Miss Ingram. She, too, was attired in oriental fashion: a crimson scarf tied sash-like around the waist: an embroidered handkerchief knotted about her temples, her beautifully moulded arms bare, one of them upraised in the action of supporting a pitcher, poised gracefully on her head. Both her cast of form and feature, her complexion and her general air, suggested the idea of some Israelitish princess of the patriarchial days; and such was doubtless the character she intended to represent.

She approached the basin, and bent over it as if to fill her pitcher; she again lifted it to her head. The personage on the well-brink now seemed to accost her, to make some request: 'She hasted, let down her pitcher on her hand, and gave him to drink.' From the bosom of his robe he then produced a casket, opened it, and showed magnificent bracelets and earrings; she acted astonishment and admiration; kneeling, he laid the treasure at her feet; incredulity and delight were expressed by her looks and gestures; the stranger fastened the bracelets on her arms and the rings in her ears. It was Eliezer and Rebecca: the camels only were wanting.

The divining party again laid their heads together: apparently they could not agree about the word or syllable the scene illustrated. Colonel Dent, their spokesman, demanded, 'the tableau of the whole'; whereupon the curtain again descended.

A Ball, a Game of Charades and Christmas Baking

On its third rising, only a portion of the drawing room was disclosed, the rest being concealed behind a screen, hung with some sort of dark and coarse drapery. The marble basin was removed; in its place stood a deal table and a kitchen chair: these objects were visible by a very dim light proceeding from a horn lantern, the wax candles being all extinguished.

Amidst this sordid scene, sat a man with his clenched hands resting on his knees, and his eyes bent on the ground. I knew Mr Rochester (his coat hanging loose from one arm, as if it had been almost torn from his back in a scuffle), the desperate and scowling countenance, the rough, bristling hair might well have disguised him. As he moved, a chain clanked; to his wrist were attached fetters.

'Bridewell!' exclaimed Colonel Dent, and the charade was solved.

A sufficient interval having elapsed for the performers to resume their ordinary costume, they re-entered the dining-room. Mr Rochester led in Miss Ingram; she was complimenting him on his acting.

'Do you know,' said she, 'that, of the three characters, I liked you in the last best? Oh, had you but lived a few years earlier, what a gallant gentleman highwayman you would have made!'

'Is all the soot washed from my face?' he asked, turning it towards her.

'Alas, yes: the more's the pity! Nothing could be more becoming to your complexion than that ruffian's rouge.'

'You would like a hero of the road then?'

'An English hero of the road would be the next best thing to an Italian bandit; and that could only be surpassed by a Levantine pirate.'

'Well, whatever I am, remember you are my wife; we were married an hour since, in the presence of all these witnesses.' She giggled and her colour rose.

'Now, Dent,' continued Mr Rochester, 'it's your turn.' And as the other party withdrew, he and his band took the vacated seats.

The final piece is full of cosy domesticity, with Jane planning to clean and bake in the traditional style to welcome her seasonal guests. Here she has left Thornfield Hall with all its grudging hospitality, and moved to Moor House, where she is made welcome by her cousins, Diana, Mary and St John. It is while she is there that she comes into a legacy. As Christmas approaches she returns again to Moor House, with her legacy, deciding to give them all a most wonderful Christmas gift – a share in her legacy, with which she decorates and furnishes the house in a bright modern way, then sets about the traditional Christmas baking in readiness for the homecoming of Diana and Mary:

It was near Christmas by the time all was settled: the season of general holiday approached. I now closed Morton school, taking care that the parting should not be barren on my side. Good fortune opens the hand as well as the heart wonderfully; and to give somewhat when we have largely received, is but to afford a vent to the unusual ebullition of the sensations. I had long felt with pleasure that many of my rustic scholars liked me, and when we parted, that consciousness was confirmed: they manifested their affection plainly and strongly. Deep was my gratification to find I had really a place in their unsophisticated hearts: I promised them that never a week should pass in future that I did not visit them, and give them an hour's teaching in their school...

'Do you consider you have got your reward for a season of exertion?' asked Mr Rivers, when they were gone. 'Does not the consciousness of having done some real good in your day and generation give pleasure?'

'Doubtless... But I could not go on forever so: I want to enjoy my own faculties as well as to cultivate those of other people. I must enjoy them now; don't recall either my mind or my body to the school; I am out of it and disposed for full holiday.'

He looked grave, 'What now? What sudden eagerness is this you evince? What are you going to do?'

'To be active: as active as I can... Diana and Mary will be at home in a week, and I want to have everything in order against their arrival.'.... 'My first aim will be to clean down (do you comprehend the full force of the expression?) – to clean down Moor House from chamber to cellar; my next to rub it up with beeswax, oil, and an indefinite number of cloths, till it glitters again; my third, to arrange every chair, table, bed, carpet, with mathematical precision, afterwards I shall go near to ruin you with coals and peat to keep up good fires in every room, and lastly, the two days preceeding that on which your sisters are expected will be devoted by Hannah and me to such a beating of eggs, sorting of currants, grating of spices, compounding of Christmas cakes, chopping up of materials for mince pies, and solemnizing of other culinary rites, as words can convey but an inadequate notion of to the uninitiated like you. My purpose, in short, is to have all things in an absolutely perfect state of readiness for Diana and Mary before next Thursday; and my ambition is to give them a beau ideal of a welcome when they come....'

Happy at Moor House I was, and hard I worked; and so did Hannah: she was charmed to see how jovial I could be amidst the bustle of a house turned topsy-turvy – how I could brush, and dust, and clean, and cook. And really, after a day or two of confusion worse confounded, it was delightful, by degrees to invoke order from the chaos ourselves had made.... When all was finished I thought Moor House as complete a model of bright, modest snugness within, as it was, at this season, a specimen of wintry waste and desert dreariness without.

The eventful Thursday at length came. They were expected about dark, and ere dusk fires were lit upstairs and below; the kitchen was in perfect trim; Hannah and I were dressed, and all was in readiness....

'They are coming. They are coming!' cried Hannah, throwing open the parlour door. At the same moment, old Carlo barked joyfully. Out I ran. It was now dark; but a rumbling of wheels was audible. Hannah soon had a lantern lit. The vehicle had stopped at the wicket; the driver opened the door; first one well-known form, then another, stepped out. In a minute I had my face under their bonnets, in contact first with Mary's soft cheek, then with Diana's flowing curls. They laughed – kissed me – then Hannah: patted Carlo, who was half wild with delight; asked eagerly if all was well; and being assured in the affirmative, hastened into the house.

They were stiff with their long and jolting drive from Whitecross, and chilled with the frosty night air; but their pleasant countenances expanded to the cheerful firelight. While the driver brought in the boxes, they demanded St John. At this moment he advanced from the parlour. They both threw their arms round his neck at once. He gave each one a quiet kiss, said in a low tone a few words of welcome, stood a while to be talked to, and then intimating that he supposed they would soon rejoin him in the parlour, withdrew there as to a place of refuge.

I had lit their candles to go upstairs, but Diana had first to give hospitable orders respecting the driver; this done, both

A Ball, a Game of Charades and Christmas Baking

followed me. They were delighted with the renovation and decorations of their rooms; with the new drapery, and fresh carpets, and rich-tinted china vases: they expressed their gratification ungrudgingly. I had the pleasure of feeling that my arrangements met their wishes exactly, and what I had done added a vivid charm to their joyous return home.

Sweet was that evening. My cousins, full of exhilaration, were so eloquent in narrative and comment, that their fluency covered St John's taciturnity: he was sincerely glad to see his sisters; but in their glow of fervour and flow of joy he could not sympathize. The event of the day – that is, the return of Diana and Mary – pleased him; but the accompaniments of that event, the glad tumult, the garrulous glee of reception, irked him: I saw he wished the calmer morrow was come....

I am afraid the whole of the ensuing week tried his patience. It was Christmas week: we took to no settled employment, but spent it in a sort of merry domestic dissipation. The air of the moors, the freedom of home, the dawn of prosperity, acted on Diana and Mary's spirits like some life-giving elixir: they were gay from morning till noon, and from noon till night. They could always talk; and their discourse, witty, pithy, original, had such charms for me, that I preferred listening to, and sharing in it, to do anything else. St John did not rebuke our vivacity; but he escaped from it; he was seldom in the house; his parish was large, the population scattered, and he found daily business in visiting the sick and poor in its different districts.

The Pantomime

WILLIAM MAKEPEACE THACKERAY

I pity a man who can't appreciate a Pantomime Overture. Children do not like it: they say, 'Hang it, I wish the Pantomime would begin'; but for us it is always a pleasant moment of reflection and enjoyment. It is not difficult music to understand.

Of Pantomime Music I am a delighted connoisseur. Perhaps it is because you meet so many old friends in these compositions consorting together in the queerest manner, and occasioning numberless pleasant surprises. Hark! There goes 'Old Dan Tucker' wandering into 'The Groves of Blarney'; our friends the 'Scots wha hae wi' Wallace bled' march rapidly down 'Wapping old stairs' from which the 'figlia del Reggimento' comes bounding briskly, when she is met, embraced, and carried off by 'Billy Taylor', that brisk young fellow.

All this while you are thinking with a faint, sickly, kind of hope, that perhaps the Pantomime may be a good one, something like, 'Harlequin and the Golden Orange Tree' which you recollect in your youth.

... Lives there the man with soul so dead, the being ever so blasé, and travel worn, who does not feel some shock and thrill still: just at that moment when the bell (the dear

The Pantomime

familiar bell of your youth) begins to tingle, and the curtain to rise, and the large shoes and ankles, the flesh coloured leggings, the crumpled knees, the gorgeous robes and masks, finally, of the actors ranged on the stage to shout the opening chorus?

All round the house you hear a great gasping a-ha-a from a thousand children's throats. Enjoyment is going to give place to Hope. Desire is about to be realized. O you blind little brats! Clap your hands and crane over the boxes, and open your eyes with happy wonder! Clap your hands now. In three weeks time the Reverend Doctor Swishtail expects the return of his young friends to Sugarcane school!

A Christmas Remembered

AN EXTRACT FROM *JANE EYRE* BY CHARLOTTE BRONTË

Early on, Jane remembers being, 'the most wicked and abandoned child ever reared,' so badly treated was she. This short extract recalls a childhood Christmas, when, excluded from everything, she looks on. . . .

Christmas and New Year had been celebrated at Gateshead with the usual festive cheer; presents had been interchanged, dinners and evening parties given. From every enjoyment I was, of course, excluded: my share of the gaiety consisted in witnessing the daily apparelling of Eliza and Georgiana, and seeing them descend to the drawing room, dressed out in thin muslin frocks and scarlet sashes, with hair elaborately ringleted; and afterwards, in listening to the sounds of the piano or the harp being played below, to the passing to and fro of the butler and footman, to the jingling of glass and china as refreshments were handed, to the broken hum of conversation as the drawing room doors opened and closed. When tired of this occupation, I would retire from the stairhead to the solitary and silent nursery: there, though somewhat sad, I was not miserable. To speak truth, I had not the least wish to go into company, for in company I was very rarely noticed: and if Bessie had been but kind and companionable, I would have deemed it a treat to spend the evenings quietly with her, instead of passing them under the formidable eye of Mrs Reed, in a room full of ladies and gentlemen. But Bessie, as soon as she had dressed her young ladies, used to take herself off to the lively regions of the kitchen and housekeeper's room, generally bearing the candle along with her. I then sat, with my doll on my knee, till the fire got low, glancing round occasionally to make sure that nothing worse than myself haunted the shadowy room; and when the embers sank to a dull red, I undressed hastily, tugging at the knots and strings as best I might, and sought shelter from the cold and darkness in my crib. To this crib I always took my doll; human beings must love something, and, in the dearth of worthier objects of affection, I contrived to find a pleasure in loving and cherishing a faded graven image, shabby as a miniature scarecrow. It puzzles me now to remember with what absurd sincerity I doted on this little toy, half fancying it alive and capable of sensation. I could not sleep unless it was folded in my nightgown; and when it lay there safe and warm, I was comparatively happy, believing it to be happy likewise.

Long did the hours seem while I waited the departure of the company, and listened for the sound of Bessie's step on the stairs. Sometimes she would come up in the interval to seek her thimble or her scissors, or perhaps to bring me something by way of supper – a bun or a cheese-cake – then she would sit on the bed while I ate it, and when I had finished, she would tuck the clothes around me, and twice she kissed me, and said, 'Good-night Miss Jane.' When thus gentle, Bessie seemed to me the best, prettiest, kindest being in the world, and I wished most intensely that she would always be so pleasant and amiable, and never push me about, or scold, or task me un-reasonably, as she was too often wont to do.

The Mahogany Tree

WILLIAM MAKEPEACE THACKERAY

Charlotte Brontë and Thackeray were to become literary friends; of him she wrote to her publisher, Mr Smith, in 1850: 'Thackeray still proves himself greater when he is weary than other writers are when they are fresh' ... and Thackeray wrote admiringly about her after her death. Here is a little-known work of his, a rather unusual Christmas poem. The mahogany tree certainly will not grow in our clime, and Thackeray was most probably referring to the mahogany dining table found in most Victorian homes, or possibly, but less likely I think, a large mahogany fire surround.

> Christmas is here;
> Winds whistle shrill,
> Icy and chill:
> Little care we,
> Little we fear
> Weather without,
> Sheltered about
> The Mahogany Tree.

The Mahogany Tree

Commoner greens,
Ivy and Oaks,
Poets, in jokes,
Sing, do you see:
Good fellow's shins
Here, boys, are found,
Twisting around
The Mahogany Tree.
Once on the boughs
Birds of rare plume
Sang, in its bloom:
Night birds are we;
Here we carouse,
Singing, like them,
Perched round the stem
Of the jolly old tree.

Here let us sport,
Boys, as we sit;
Laughter, and wit,
Flashing so free,
Life is but short –
When we are gone,
Let them sing on,
Round the old tree.
Evenings we knew,
Happy as this;
Faces we miss,
Pleasant to see.
Kind hearts and true,
Gentle and just,
Peace to your dust!
We sing round the tree.

Care, like a dun,
Lurks at the gate:
Let the dog wait;
Happy we'll be!
Drink every one;
Pile up the coals,
Fill the red bowls,
Round the old tree!

Drain we the cup. –
Friend, art afraid?
Spirits are laid
In the Red Sea.
Mantle it up;
Empty it yet;
Let us forget,
Round the old tree.

Sorrows, begone!
Life and its ills,
Duns and their bills,
Bid we to flee.
Come with the dawn
Blue-devil sprite
Leave us to-night,
Round the old tree.

Christmas Storms and Sunshine

MRS GASKELL

Mrs Elizabeth Gaskell surely deserves her place in any anthology of the Brontës. We have already mentioned her biography of Charlotte. Her own writings depict much of the Christmas of the time, in real early Victorian Dickensian style! The following story comes from the 1848 Christmas issue of *Howitt's Journal* where it first appeared, a semi-professional magazine which lasted a very short time by all accounts. Having lost a child, Mrs Gaskell wrote prolifically that year, and completed her first novel, *Mary Barton*. Her work did in fact reach the attention of the great Dickens, who published her in his own magazines, *Household Worlds* and *All the Year Round*. One might imagine Charlotte, assuming Elizabeth showed her a copy, reading her friend's story, exactly as it appears here.

In the town of – no matter where – there circulated two national newspapers no matter when. Now the 'Flying Post' was long established and respectable – alias bigoted and Tory; the 'Examiner' was spirited and intelligent – alias newfangled and democratic. Every week these newspapers contained articles abusing each other, as cross and peppery as articles could be, and evidently the production of irritated minds, although they seemed to have one stereotyped commencement – 'Though the article appearing in our last week's "Post" (or "Examiner") is below contempt, yet we have been induced,' etc etc.; and every Saturday the Radical shopkeepers shook hands together, and agreed that the 'Post' was done for by the slashing, clever 'Examiner'; while the more dignified Tories began by regretting that Johnson should think that low paper, only read by a few of the vulgar, worth wasting his wit upon; however, the 'Examiner' was at its last gasp.

It was not, though. It lived and flourished; at least it paid its way, as one of the heroes of my story could tell. He was chief compositor, or whatever title may be given to the head man of the mechanical part of a newspaper. He hardly confined himself to the department. Once or twice, unknown to the editor, when the manuscript had fallen short, he filled up the vacant space by compositions of his own; announcements of a forthcoming crop of green peas in December; a grey thrush having been seen, or a white hare, or such interesting phenomena; invented for the occasion, I must confess; but what of that? His wife always knew when to expect a little specimen of her husband's literary talent by a peculiar cough, which served as a prelude; and, judging from this encouraging sign, and the high pitched and emphatic voice in which he read them, she was inclined to think that, 'An Ode to an early Rosebud,' in the corner devoted to original poetry, and a letter in the correspondence department, signed 'Pro Bono Publico,' were her husband's writing, and to hold her head up accordingly.

I could never find out what it was that occasioned the Hodgsons to lodge in the same house as the Jenkinses, Jenkins held the same office in the Tory Paper as Hodgson did in the 'Examiner,' and, as I said before, I leave you to give it a name. But Jenkins had a proper sense of his position, and a proper reverence for all in authority, from the king down to the editor and the subeditor. He would have as soon thought of borrowing the king's crown for a night-cap, or the king's sceptre for a walking stick, as he would have thought of filling up any spare corner with any production of his own; and I think it would have even added to his contempt of Hodgson (if that were possible), had he known of the 'productions of his brain', as the latter fondly alluded to the paragraphs he inserted, when speaking to his wife.

Jenkins had a wife too. Wives were wanting to finish the completeness of the quarrel which existed one memorable Christmas week, some dozen years ago, between the two neighbours, the two compositors. And with wives, it was a very pretty, a very complete quarrel. To make the opposing parties still more equal, still more well-matched, if the Hodgsons had a baby ('such a baby! a poor, puny little thing'), Mrs Jenkins had a cat ('such a cat! a great, nasty, miowling tom-cat, that was always stealing the milk put by for little Angel's supper'). And now, having matched Greek with Greek, I must proceed to the tug of war. It was the day before Christmas; such a cold east wind! such an inky sky! such a blue-black look in people's faces, as they were driven out more than usual, to complete their purchases for the next day's festival. Before leaving home that morning, Jenkins had given some money to his wife to buy the next day's dinner.

'My dear, I wish for turkey and sausages. It must be a weakness, but I own I am partial to sausages. My deceased mother was. Such tastes are hereditary. As to the sweets – whether plum pudding or mince pies – I leave such considerations to you; I beg you only not to mind expense. Christmas comes but once a year.'

Christmas Storms and Sunshine

And again he called out from the bottom of the first flight of stairs, just close to the Hodgson's door ('such ostentatiousness,' as Mrs Hodgson observed), 'You will not forget the sausages my dear!'

'I should have liked to have something above common, Mary,' said Hodgson, as they too made their plans for the next day; 'but I think roast beef must do for us. You see love, we've a family.'

'Only one, Jem! I don't want more than roast beef, though, I'm sure. Before I went to service, my mother and me would have thought roast beef a very fine dinner.'

'Well, let's settle it, then, roast beef and a plum pudding; and now, goodbye. Mind and take care of little Tom. I thought he was a bit hoarse this morning.'

And off he went to work.

Now, it was a good while since Mrs Jenkins and Mrs Hodgson had spoken to each other, although they were quite as much in possession of the knowledge of events and opinions as though they did. Mary knew that Mrs Jenkins despised her for not having a real lace cap, which Mrs Jenkins had; and for having been a servant, which Mrs Jenkins had not; and for the occasional little pinchings which the Hodgsons were obliged to resort to, to make both ends meet, would have been very patiently endured by Mary, if she had not winced under Mrs Jenkins' knowledge of such economy. But she had her revenge. She had a child, and Mrs Jenkins had none. To have had a child, even such a puny baby as Tom, Mrs Jenkins would have worn the commonest caps, and cleaned grates, and drudged her fingers to the bone. The great unspoken disappointment in her life soured her temper, and turned her thoughts inward, and made her morbid and selfish.

'Hang that cat! he's been stealing again! he's gnawed the cold mutton in his nasty mouth till it's not fit to set before a

Christian: and I've nothing else for Jem's dinner. But I'll give it to him now I've caught him, that I will!'

So saying, Mary Hodgson caught up her husband's Sunday cane, and despite pussy's cries and scratches, she gave him such a beating as she hoped might cure him of his thievish propensities; when, lo! and behold, Mrs Jenkins stood in the door with a face of bitter wrath.

'Aren't you ashamed of yourself, ma'am, to abuse a poor dumb animal, ma'am? He only follows the nature which God has given, ma'am; and it's a pity your nature, ma'am, which I've heard is of the stingy saving species, does not make you shut your cupboard door a little closer. There is such a thing as law for brute animals. I'll ask Mr Jenkins, but I don't think them Radicals have done away with that law yet, for all their reform bills, ma'am. My poor precious love of a Tommy, is he hurt? and is his leg broke for taking a mouthful of scraps as most people would give away to a beggar – if he'd take 'em!' wound up Mrs Jenkins, casting a contemptuous look on the remnant of a scrag end of mutton.

Mary felt very angry and very guilty. For she really pitied the poor limping animal as he crept up to his mistress, and there lay down to bemoan himself; she wished she had not beaten him so hard, for it certainly was her own careless way of never shutting the cupboard door that had tempted him to his fault. But the sneer at her little bit of mutton turned her penitence to fresh wrath, and she shut the door in Mrs Jenkins' face, as she stood caressing her cat in the lobby, with such a bang, that it wakened little Tom, and he began to cry.

Everything was to go wrong with Mary today. Now baby was awake, who was to take her husband's dinner to the office? She took the child in her arms and tried to hush him off to sleep again, and as she sang she cried, she could hardly tell why – a sort of reaction from her violent angry feelings.

She wished she had never beaten the poor cat; she wondered if his leg was really broken. What would her mother say if she knew how cross and cruel her little Mary was getting? If she should live to beat her child in one of her angry fits?

It was of no use lullabying when she sobbed so; it must be given up, and she must just carry her baby in her arms, and take him with her to the office, for it was long past dinnertime. So she pared the mutton carefully, although by so doing she reduced the meat to an infinitesimal quantity, and taking the baked potatoes out of the oven she popped them, piping hot, into her basket, with the etceteras of plate, butter, salt, and knife and fork.

It was, indeed, a bitter wind. She bent against it as she ran, and the flakes of snow were sharp and cutting as ice. Baby cried all the way, though she cuddled him up in her shawl. Then her husband had made his appetite up for a potato pie, and (literary man that he was) his body got so much the better of his mind, that he looked rather black at the cold mutton. Mary had no appetite for her own dinner when she arrived at home again. So, after she had tried to feed baby, and he had fretfully refused to take his bread and milk, she laid him down as usual on his quilt, surrounded by playthings, while she sidled away, and chopped suet for the next day's pudding.

Early in the afternoon a parcel came, done up first in brown paper, then in such a white, grass bleached, sweet-smelling towel, and a note from her dear, dear mother; in which quaint writing she endeavoured to tell her daughter that she was not forgotten at Christmas time; but that, learning that Farmer Burton was killing his pig, she had made interest for some of his famous pork, out of which she had manufactured some sausages, and flavoured them just as Mary used to like when she lived at home.

'Dear, dear mother!' said Mary to herself. 'There never was anyone like her for remembering other folk. What rare sausages she used to make! Home things have a smack with 'em no bought things can ever have. Set them up with their sausages! I've a notion if Mrs Jenkins had ever tasted mother's she'd have no fancy for them townmade things Fanny took in just now.'

And so she went on thinking about home, till the smiles and the dimples came out again at the remembrance of that pretty cottage, which would look green even now in the depth of winter, with its pyracanthus, and its holly-bushes, and the great Portugal laurel that was her mother's pride. And the back path through the orchard to Farmer Burton's, how well she remembered it! The bushels of unripe apples she had picked up there and distributed among his pigs, till he had scolded her for giving them so much green trash!

She was interrupted – her baby (I call him a baby, because his father and mother did, and because he was so little for his age, but I rather think he was eighteen months old) had fallen asleep some time before among his playthings; an uneasy, restless sleep; but of which Mary had been thankful, as his morning's nap had been too short, and as she was so busy. But now he began to make such a strange crowing noise, just like a chair drawn heavily and gratingly across a kitchen floor! His eyes were open, but expressive of nothing but pain.

'Mother's darling!' said Mary in terror, lifting him up. 'Baby, try not to make that noise. Hush, hush, darling; what hurts him?' But the noise came worse and worse.

'Fanny! Fanny!' Mary called in mortal fright, for her baby was almost black with his gasping breath and she had no-one to ask for aid or sympathy but her landlady's daughter, a little girl of twelve or thirteen, who attended to the house in her mother's absence, as daily cook in gentlemen's families. Fanny was more especially considered the attendant of the upstairs lodgers (who paid for the use of the kitchen, 'for Mr Jenkins could not abide the smell of meat cooking') but just now she was fortunately sitting at her afternoon's work of darning socks, and hearing Mrs Hodgson's cry of terror, she ran to her sitting room, and understood the case at a glance.

'He's got the croup! O Mrs Hodgson, he'll die sure as fate. Little brother had it, and he died in no time. The doctor said he could do nothing for him, it had gone too far. He said if we'd put him in a warm bath at first, it might have saved him; but bless you! he was never half as bad as your baby.' Unconsciously there mingled in her statement some of the child's love of producing an effect; but the increasing danger was clear enough.

'Fanny, what is the fire like in the kitchen? Speak.'

'Mother told me to screw it up, and throw some slack on as soon as Mrs Jenkins had done with it, and so I did. It's very low and black. But, oh! Mrs Hodgson, let me run for the doctor – I cannot bear to hear him, it's so like little brother . . .'

Mrs Jenkins, having cooked her husband's snug little dinner, to which he came home; having told him her story of pussy's beating, at which he was justly and dignifiably indignant, saying it was all of a piece with that abusive 'Examiner'; having received the sausages, and turkey and mince pies, which her husband had ordered; and cleaned up the room, and prepared everything for tea, and coaxed and duly bemoaned her cat (who had pretty nearly forgotten his beating, but very much enjoyed the petting); having done all these and many other things, Mrs Jenkins sat down to get up the real lace cap. Every thread was pulled out separately, and carefully stretched: when, what was that?

Outside in the street, a chorus of piping children's voices sang the old carol she had heard a hundred times in the days of her youth:

'As Joseph was a walking he heard an angel sing,
"This night shall be born our heavenly King.
He neither shall be bornen in housen nor in hall,
Nor in the place of Paradise, but in an ox's stall.

He neither shall be clothed in purple nor in pall
But all in fairest linen as was babies all:
He neither shall be rocked in silver nor in gold,
But in the wooden cradle that rocks on the mould. Amen."'

She got up and went to the window. There below, stood the group of black little figures, relieved against the snow, which now enveloped everything. 'For old sake's sake' as she phrased it, she counted out a half pence apiece for the singers, out of the copper bag, and threw them down below.

... Like Mary Hodgson she began to think over long past days, on softening remembrances of the dead and gone, on words long forgotten, on holy stories heard at her mother's knee.

'I cannot think what's come over me tonight,' said she, half aloud, recovering herself by the sound of her own voice, from her train of thought. – 'My head goes wandering on them old times. I'm sure more texts have come into my head within this last half-hour, than I've thought on for years and years. I hope I'm not going to die. Folks say, thinking too much on the dead betokens we're going to join 'em; I should be loth to go just yet – such a fine turkey as we've got for dinner tomorrow too!'

Knock, knock, knock, at the door, as fast as knuckles could go. And then, as if the comer could not wait, the door was opened, and Mary Hodgson stood there white as death.

'Mrs Jenkins! Oh, your kettle is boiling, thank God! Let me have the water for my baby, for the love of God! He's got croup and is dying!'

Mrs Jenkins turned on her chair with a wooden, inflexible look on her face, that (between ourselves) her husband knew and dreaded for all his pomposity.

'I'm sorry I can't oblige you, ma'am; my kettle is wanted for my husband's tea. Don't be afeared Tommy, Mrs Hodgson won't venture to intrude herself where she's not desired. You'd better send for the doctor ma'am, instead of wasting your time wringing your hands, ma'am – my kettle is engaged.'

Mary clasped her hands together with passionate force, but spoke not word of entreaty to that wooden face – that sharp, determined voice; but as she turned away, she prayed for strength to face the coming trial, and strength to forgive Mrs Jenkins.

Mrs Jenkins watched her go away meekly, as one who has no hope, and then she turned upon herself as sharply as she ever did on anyone else.

'What a brute I am, Lord forgive me! What's my husband's tea to a baby's life? In croup too, where time is everything. You crabbed old vixen you! – anyone may know you never had a child!'

She was downstairs (kettle in hand) before she had finished her upbraiding; and when in Mrs Hodgson's room, she rejected all thanks (Mary had no voice for many words) saying, stiffly, 'I do it for the poor babby's sake, ma'am, hoping he may live to have mercy on poor dumb beasts, if he does forget to lock his cupboards.'

But she did everything, and more than Mary, in her young experience, could have thought of. She prepared the warm bath and tried it with her husband's own thermometer (Mr Jenkins was as punctual as clockwork in noting down the temperature of every day). She let his mother place her baby in the tub, still preserving the same rigid, affronted aspect, and then she went upstairs without a word. Mary longed to ask her to stay, but dared not; though, when she left the room, the tears chased each other down her cheeks faster than ever. Poor young mother! how she counted the minutes till the doctor should come. But before he came, down again stalked Mrs Jenkins with something in her hand.

'I've seen many of these croup-fits, which, I take it you've not, ma'am. Mustard plaisters is very sovereign, put on the throat; I've been up and made one, ma'am, and, by your leave, I'll put it on the poor little fellow.'

Mary could not speak, but she signed her grateful assent.

It began to smart while they still kept silence; and he looked up at his mother as if seeking courage from her looks to bear the stinging pain; but she was softly crying to see him suffer, and her want of courage reacted upon him, and he began to sob aloud. Instantly Mrs Jenkins' apron was up, hiding her face: 'Peep-bo, baby,' said she, as merrily as she could. His little face brightened, and his mother, having once got the cue, the two women kept the little fellow amused, until his plaister had taken effect.

'He's better – oh, Mrs Jenkins, look at his eyes! how different! and he breathes quite softly.'

As Mary spoke thus, the doctor entered. He examined his patient. Baby was really better.

'It has been a sharp attack, but the remedies you have applied have been worth all the Pharmacopoeia an hour later. I shall send a powder, etc. etc.'

Mrs Jenkins stayed to hear this opinion; and (her heart wonderfully more easy) was going to leave the room, when

Christmas Storms and Sunshine

Mary seized her hand and kissed it; she could not speak her gratitude. Mrs Jenkins looked affronted and awkward, and as if she must go upstairs and wash her hand directly.

But in spite of these sour looks, she came softly down, an hour or so afterwards, to see how baby slept.

The little gentleman slept well after the fright he had given his friends; and on Christmas morning, when Mary awoke and looked at the sweet little pale face lying on her arm, she could hardly realise the danger he had been in.

When she came down, later than usual, she found the household in commotion. What do you think had happened? Why, pussy had been traitor to his best friend and eaten up some of Mr Jenkins' own special sausages; and gnawed and rumbled the rest so, that they were not fit to be eaten! There were no bounds to that cat's appetite! he would have eaten his own father if he had been tender enough. And now Mr Jenkins stormed and cried, 'Hang the cat!'

'Christmas Day too! and all the shops shut! What was turkey without sausages?' gruffly asked Mr Jenkins.

'O, Jem!' whispered Mary, 'hearken what a piece of work he's making about sausages – I should like to take Mrs Jenkins up some of mother's; they're twice as good as bought sausages.'

'I see no objection, my dear. Sausages do not involve intimacies, else his politics are what I can no ways respect.'

'But, oh, Jem, if you had seen her last night about baby! I'm sure she may scold me forever and I'll not answer. I'd even make her cat welcome to the sausages.' The tears gathered in Mary's eyes as she kissed her boy.

'Better take 'em upstairs my dear, and give them to the cat's mistress.' And Jem chuckled at his saying.

Mary put them on a plate, but still she loitered.

'What must I say, Jem? I never know.'

'Say – I hope you'll accept these sausages, as my mother – no, that's not grammar, – say what comes uppermost, Mary, it will sure to be right.'

So Mary carried them upstairs, and knocked at the door, and when told to 'come in', she looked very red, but went up to Mrs Jenkins, saying, 'Please take these, Mother made them', and went away before an answer could be given.

Just as Hodgson was ready to go to church, Mrs Jenkins came downstairs and called Fanny. In a minute the latter entered the Hodgsons' room, and delivered Mr and Mrs Jenkins' compliments, and they would be particularly glad if Mr and Mrs Hodgson would eat their dinner with them.

'And carry baby upstairs in a shawl, to be sure,' added Mrs Jenkins' voice in the passage, close to the door, whither she had followed her messenger. There was no discussing the matter, with the certainty of every word being overheard.

Mary looked anxiously at her husband. She remembered his saying he did not approve of Mr Jenkins' politics.

'Do you think it would do for baby?' asked he.

'Oh, yes,' answered she eagerly; 'I would wrap him up so warm.'

'And I've got our room up to sixty-five already, for all it's so frosty,' added the voice outside.

Now, how do you think they settled the matter? The very best way in the world. Mr and Mrs Jenkins came down into the Hodgsons' room and dined there. Turkey at the top, roast beef at the bottom, sausages at one side, potatoes at the other. Second course plum pudding at the top, mince pies at the bottom.

And after dinner, Mrs Jenkins would have baby on her knee, and he seemed quite to take to her; she declared he was admiring the real lace on her cap, but Mary thought (though she did not say so) that he was pleased by her kind looks and coaxing words. Then he was wrapped up and carried carefully upstairs to tea, in Mrs Jenkins' room. And after tea, Mrs Jenkins, and Mary, and her husband, found out each other's mutual liking for music, and sat singing old glees and catches, till I don't know what o'clock, without one word of politics or newspapers.

Before they parted, Mary coaxed pussy on her knee; for Mrs Jenkins would not part from baby, who was sleeping on her lap.

'When you're busy bring him to me, do now, it will be a real favour. I know you must have a deal to do, with another coming; let him come up to me. I'll take the greatest care of him; pretty darling, how sweet he looks when he's asleep!'

When the couples were once more alone, the husbands unburdened their minds to their wives.

Mr Jenkins said to his – 'Do you know, Burgess tried to make me believe Hodgson was such a fool to put paragraphs into the 'Examiner' now and then; but I see he knows his place, and has too much sense to do any such thing.'

Hodgson said – 'Mary, love, I almost fancy from Jenkins' way of speaking (so much civiler than I expected), he guesses I wrote that "Pro Bono" and the "Rosebud" – at any rate, I've no objection to your naming it, if the subject should come uppermost; I should like him to know I'm a literary man.'

Well! I've ended my tale; I hope you don't think it too long; but, before I go, just let me say one thing.

If any of you have any quarrels, or misunderstandings, or coolnesses, or cold shoulders, or shynesses, or tiffs, or miffs, or huffs, with anyone else, just make friends before Christmas – you will be so much merrier if you do.

I ask it of you for the sake of that old angelic song, heard so many years ago by the shepherds, keeping watch by night, on Bethlehem Heights.

Annuals, Albums and Christmas Art

Did the Brontës extend their search for fame to art? Or were the distinctly greetings-card-style images they painted purely for their own pleasure, or as gifts to friends? The following research opens the question.

That all of the Brontë children were artists, with varying degrees of talent, was obvious. They drew, painted and sketched all their lives. Branwell created most of the characters for the children's juvenile stories. Emily enjoyed sketching animals, especially the family pets. Charlotte seems to have gone in for the classical look of the day, producing pastoral scenes, and classic heads galore, while much of Anne's work was typical of the popular greetings card images of the day, cottages, churches and country scenes in delicate watercolours, often on specially purchased cards with fancy borders – most of the Brontë artwork is at the Brontë Museum in Haworth today, and reveals some surprises.

Within the field of Christmas illustration, there were many attempts by many worthy people of the day. Young ladies with leisure on their hands and sometimes real talent, such as Kate Greenaway; titled ladies whose main claim to fame were their elaborate houseparties, who felt that life had somehow left them behind; well known authors and poets and even Royal Academicians, all found this new art form intriguing. From its infancy to the fruition of the first commercial Christmas card in 1842, it was a discipline which attracted the artist, the collector and the copyist alike.

At first, colour printing was prohibitively expensive. The term 'Penny Plain, Tuppence Coloured' grew from the custom of producing card sheets for games, particularly the game of Twelfth Night Characters, as either plain engravings, or coloured with hand stencils. These produced a very rough and uneven colouring, as the colours were put on in blocks. Thus the reproduction of artwork from such would-be artists as the Brontës was a non-starter in their early years. However, all of the Brontës, with the exception of Charlotte, died before the need for card illustrators began in earnest. It would be towards the end of Charlotte's life, in 1853, before any real headway was made.

Pioneer printing techniques such as the Baxter, which blended engraving with a colour technique; and later, in the late 1850s the even cheaper chromolithography patented in Bavaria by Raphael Tuck, together with the emergence of the penny postal service meant that the custom of giving a card was within the grasp of many – thus the need for ever new and different artwork was paramount. Within forty years of its innovation, this industry was to have over 173,000 images already in publication, and many thousands more on the stocks. Some of these designs were private family sketches and watercolours bought in by the publishers from families of literary and artistic note. So it is not impossible that a card published by, say, Hildesheimer in the 1870s, might have been one of Anne Brontë's scenes from the 1830s.

Begun and developed spasmodically during the 1840s, the Christmas card grew out of the personal greetings cards which people painted and left on silver platters at the homes of friends and neighbours. It was the custom to make greetings cards, and then visit one's acquaintances to deliver these, either in person, or if the recipient was not at home, they were left, like a calling card. It was considered good taste to paint or script these cards oneself to show a degree of personality and thought in the greeting. This was, of course, in the days *before* the commercial greetings card and the techniques described became so fashionable.

Many of the designs executed by the Brontë sisters particularly, would have lent themselves to this art form, had they come a few years later. But by the time the cheaper process of chromolithography was established, all the sisters had gone. Whether they created the designs to leave on the silver salvers of their acquaintances is not known, unfortunately. Many designs, which could have been Brontë originals, appeared as greetings cards during the mid to late Victorian period, and it would be easy to ask the question, 'Did someone sell the girls' designs to a greetings card publisher posthumously?' We shall never know that answer.

There is a slight coincidence here however, in that at least two of the small embossed cards which have Brontë paintings on them, bear the name of Christmas card publishers, those of De la Rue, and Dobbs. Both publishers were among the early pioneers of greetings card publication, and it is conceivable that they could have obtained Brontë designs to reproduce, in those days before the copyright laws prevented such things, within a decade of the death of Charlotte.

The girls obviously used commercially produced blank cards which were designed for the 'silver salver card', which by its indication would make the probability that the girls did at least make greetings cards to give, very real.

Painstaking investigation has revealed, sadly, no proof to substantiate this line of research, other than the little cards in the Brontë Museum, with the publishers' names.

Annuals, Albums and Christmas Art

What is true, however, is that Charlotte, at least, painted the images which she and her sisters found in the Christmas annuals, whether for their own pleasure; to give to their friends and acquaintances in the time-honoured way; or with perhaps some secret hope of ever being published in one of them would be impossible to say. Certainly the girls had several of these little books to copy from, expensive though they were.

These early annuals were small books priced to reach the middle classes, often with beautifully written stories and articles on many subjects, and well illustrated with tissue-guarded steel engravings. Popular were Forget-me-not, Atlantic Souvenir (an American publication) and Peter Parley Annual. There was hardly any Christmas content, and most were suitable for Sunday reading, when only religious or 'edifying' material could be read!

Such annuals were usually placed on tables for the convenience of family and visitor alike, together with the fashionable album. This, during the early part of the nineteenth century, was a high quality, often morocco and brass bound volume, with highly decorated pages, sometimes with mounts for photographs, other times with blank pages for one's own decoration. As the century wore on, the pages became filled with quality chromo-lithograph illustrations, and often contained a musical box movement in the back cover. But in the Brontës' time, the quality was all in the workmanship of the bindings. In these albums, young ladies would pass the hours painting and drawing, writing verses and prose, even keeping a sort of seasonal diary. Less artistic ladies would find suitable pictures, engravings, or perhaps texts from newspapers to stick on to the pages. Patterns for lace collars, designs for sewing boxes, might be included – all things which showed the skills of the young ladies of the house. The Brontë girls all made such items.

In later years it became the fashion to create albums almost entirely filled with greetings cards, painstakingly stuck in and often with watercolour illustration around the blank areas of the page: a fashionable hobby for ladies with leisure time.

Such customs were deplored by the oft-times outspoken Thackeray, who said of them, ' . . . that unfortunate collection of deformed Zuleikas and Medoras . . . glaring caricatures of flowers, singly, in groups, in flowerpots, or with hideous deformed little cupids sporting among them . . . The "Album" is to be found invariably upon the round, rosewood, brass-inlaid drawing-room table of the middle classes, and with a couple of "Annuals" besides, which flank it on the same table, and represents the art of the house. . . .'

These were presents for the wealthy, and not usually very Christmassy at all in their content, but given and welcomed as most acceptable Christmas gifts for all that.

Into this tradition came the creatively inclined and oft frustrated Brontë children. They began writing their make-believe stories from an early age. The 'Islanders' and 'The Search after Hapiness' were completed almost before any of them were into their teens. Painstakingly written in tiny notebooks, and illustrated, they give more than a glimpse at the way the children immersed themselves into their fantasy world to escape the often miserable existence in that bleak parsonage, with only a strict puritanical aunt, and a grieving and untimely widower father to bring them up. The only affection they would have known from the time their mother died, was from their old nurse, Tabby.

It is little wonder that their early works show no Christmas content. But as they grew to adulthood, outside influences encroached, and Christmas began to appear – in their poems, their novels and less known, in their art.

The two most Christmassy pieces of artwork done by the Brontës are a passable Madonna and Child, which, at first glance appears to be after Raphael, and later research disclosed it to be, in fact, a copy of an engraving of Raphael's 'Madonna of the Fish' by Louis Schalz. This was done by Charlotte Brontë, and was probably copied again from a book or magazine. The second is a lovely 'Adoration of the Shepherds' by Branwell, apparently when he was studying painting under one William Robinson in the mid-1830s. Again, a copy of an old master.

There is a third painting copied from an original; this is 'The Link Boy' again done by Branwell during his time with Robinson. This is not essentially a Christmas picture, but the subject of link boy or lantern carrier has been used many times since as a Christmas card subject, because of the association with Christmas and coaches. The link boys carried their lanterns in front of the coaches to light the way up the drives and to the stables of the great houses.

While Branwell's Christmas imagery seems to have been from Old Masters, and Charlotte copied the romantic portraits particularly, from the story books and annuals – her freehand portraits of her family veered almost toward the 'primitive' style, Emily and Anne would have undoubtedly made good Christmas card illustrators a few decades later. Emily made very skilful portraits of the family pets, the house dog, Keeper, and her tame merlin, Hero, are particularly excellent examples. Anne's scenes were especially commercially viable for greetings cards. Charlotte was also capable of commercial quality work. She drew and painted a number of scenes with buildings, designs for workboxes, plate borders and so on.

The Magic Lantern

WILLIAM MAKEPEACE THACKERAY

I still sometimes get a degree of pleasure by hearing the voices of children in the dark, and the absurd remarks which they make as the various scenes are presented – as, in the dissolving views, Cornhill changes into Grand Cairo, as Cupid comes down with a wreath, and pops it on the head of the Duke of Wellington, as St Peter's at Rome suddenly becomes illuminated, and fireworks, not the least like real fireworks, begin to go off from Fort St-Angelo, it is certainly not unpleasant to hear the 'oo-os' of the audience, and the little children chattering in the dark.

A Tragic Christmas Tale

CHARLOTTE BRONTË

The following tale is told in *Villette* by Miss Marchmont, who, in a nostalgic mood when she confesses 'I love Memory tonight,' she tells her visitor about a love lost one Christmastide.

'My dear girl,' she said, 'one happy Christmas Eve I dressed and decorated myself, expecting my lover, very soon to be my husband, would come that night to visit me. I sat down to wait. Once more I see that moment – I see the snow-twilight stealing through the window over which the curtain was not dropped, for I designed to watch him walk up the white walk; I see and feel the soft firelight warming me, playing on my silk dress, and fitfully showing me my own young figure in a glass. I see the moon of a calm winter night float full, clear and cold, over the inky mass of shrubbery, and the silvered turf of my grounds, I wait, with some impatience in my pulse, but no doubt in my breast. The flames had died in the fire, but it was a bright mass yet; the moon was mounting high, but she was still visible from the lattice; the clock neared ten; he rarely tarried later than this, but once or twice he had been delayed so long.

'Would he for once fail me? No – not even for once; and now he was coming and coming fast – to atone for lost time. "Frank! you furious rider," I said inwardly, listening gladly, yet anxiously to his approaching gallop, "you shall be rebuked for this: I will tell you it is my neck you are putting in peril; for whatever is yours is, in a dearer and tenderer sense, mine." There he was: I saw him; but I think tears were in my eyes; my sight was so confused. I saw the horse; I heard it stamp – I saw at least a mass; I heard a clamour. Was it a horse? or what heavy, dragging thing was it, crossing, strangely dark, the lawn? How could I name that thing in the moonlight before me? or how could I utter the feeling which rose in my soul?

'I could only run out. A great animal – truly, Frank's black horse – stood trembling, panting, snorting before the door; a man held it: Frank, as I thought.

'"What is the matter?" I demanded. Thomas, my own servant, answered by saying sharply, "Go into the house, Madam." And then, calling to some other servant who came hurrying from the kitchen as if summoned by some instinct, "Ruth, take Missus into the house directly." But I was kneeling down in the snow, beside something that lay there – something that I had seen dragged along the ground – something that sighed, that groaned on my breast, as I lifted and drew it to me. He was not dead; he was not quite unconscious. I had him carried in; I refused to be ordered about and thrust from him. I was quite collected enough, not only to be my own mistress, but the mistress of others. They had begun by trying to treat me like a child, as they always do with people struck by God's hand; but I gave place to none except the surgeon; and when he had done what he could, I took my dying Frank to myself. He had strength to fold me in his arms; he had power to speak my name; he heard me as I prayed over him very softly; he felt me as I tenderly and fondly comforted him.

"'Maria,' he said, "I am dying in Paradise." He spent his last breath in faithful words for me. When the dawn of Christmas morning broke, my Frank was with God.

'And that', she went on, 'happened thirty years ago.'

Charlotte's Last Spice Cake

Charlotte married finally in 1854. She and her husband enjoyed many walks on the moors near their home, and in the winter, even the inclement weather of the bleak Yorkshire moors did not quell her love. On 29 November she wrote:

I intended to have written a line yesterday, but just as I was sitting down for the purpose, Arthur called for me to take a walk. We set off not intending to go far; but, though wild and cloudy, it was fair in the morning; when we had gone about half a mile on the moors, Arthur suggested the idea of the waterfall; after the melting snow, he said it would be fine. I had often wished to see it in its winter power, – so we walked on. It was fine indeed; a perfect torrent racing over the rocks, white and beautiful! It began to rain while we were watching it, and we returned home under a streaming sky. However, I enjoyed the walk inexpressibly, and would not have missed the spectacle on any account.

However, the soaking did her no good, and she developed a cold, which lingered, making her thin and weak. Mrs Gaskell, in her biography of Charlotte, takes up the tale:

On Christmas-day she and her husband walked to the poor old woman (whose calf she had been set to seek in former and less happy days), carrying with them a great spice-cake to make glad her heart. On Christmas-day many a humble meal in Haworth was made more plentiful by her gifts.

It was to be the last time Charlotte would go out with her Christmas dole to the people of Haworth. Early in the New Year she had a renewed attack, caused no doubt by her frequent walking out in thin shoes upon the damp ground, and breathing in the damp Yorkshire air, so notoriously bad for the chest. On March 31st 1855, she breathed her last, and so did the child she believed she carried.

The Wassail Cup of 'Old October'

A SECOND EXTRACT FROM *VILLETTE*
BY CHARLOTTE BRONTË

Cheerful as my godmother naturally was, and entertaining as, for our sakes, she made a point of being, there was no true enjoyment that evening at La Terrasse, till, through the wild howl of the winter night, was heard the signal sounds of arrival. How often, while women and girls sit warm at snug firesides, their hearts and imaginations are doomed to divorce from the comfort surrounding their persons, forced out by night to wander through dark ways, to dare stress of weather, to contend with the snow-blast, to wait at lonely gates and stiles in wildest storms, watching and listening to see and hear the father, the son, the husband coming home.

Father and son came at last to the chateau: for the Count de Bassompierre that night accompanied Dr Bretton. I know not which of our trio heard the horses first; the asperity, the violence of the weather warranted our running down into the hall to meet and greet the two riders as they came in; but they warned us to keep our distance: both were white – two moving mountains of snow; and indeed Mrs Bretton, seeing their condition, ordered them instantly to the kitchen, prohibiting them, at their peril, from setting foot on her carpeted staircase till they had severally put off

The Wassail Cup of 'Old October'

that mask of Old Christmas they now affected. Into the kitchen, however, we could not help following them: it was a large old Dutch kitchen, picturesque and pleasant. The little white Countess danced in a circle about her equally white sire, clapping her hands, and crying, –

'Papa, papa, you look like an enormous Polar bear.'

The bear shook himself, and the little sprite fled far from the frozen shower. Back she came, however, laughing, and eager to aid in removing the arctic disguise. The Count, at last issuing from his dreadnought, threatened to overwhelm her with it as with an avalanche.

'Come then,' said she, bending to invite the fall, and when it was playfully advanced above her head, bounding out of reach like some little chamois.

Her movements had the supple softness, the velvet grace of a kitten; her laugh was clearer than the ring of silver and crystal: as she took her sire's cold hands and rubbed them, and stood on tiptoe to reach his lips for a kiss, there seemed to shine round her a halo of loving delight. The grave and reverend signior looked down at her as men do look on what is the apple of their eye.

'Mrs Bretton,' said he; 'what am I to do with this daughter or daughterling of mine? She neither grows in wisdom nor in stature. Don't you find her pretty much as nearly the child as she was ten years ago?'

'She cannot be more the child than this great boy of mine,' said Mrs Bretton, who was in conflict with her son about some change of dress she deemed advisable, and which he resisted. He stood leaning against the Dutch dresser, laughing and keeping her at arm's length.

'Come, mama,' said he, 'by way of compromise, and to secure for us inward as well as outward warmth, let us have a Christmas wassail-cup, and toast Old England here, on the hearth.'

So, while the Count stood by the fire, and Paulina Mary still danced to and fro – happy in the liberty of the wide, hall-like kitchen – Mrs Bretton herself instructed Martha to spice and heat the wassail bowl, and, pouring the draught into a Bretton flagon, it was served round, reaming hot, by means of a small silver vessel, which I recognised as Graham's christening cup.

'Here's to Auld Lang Syne!' said the Count; holding the glancing cup on high. Then, looking at Mrs Bretton:

'We twa ha' paidlet i' the burn
Fra morning-sun till dine,
But seas between us braid ha' roared
Sin auld lang syne.

And Surely ye'll be your pint-stoup,
As surely I'll be mine;
And we'll taste a cup o' kindness yet
For auld lang syne.'

'Scotch! Scotch!' cried Paulina; 'papa is talking Scotch; and Scotch he is, partly. We are Home and De Bassompierre, Caledonian and Gallic.'

'And is that a Scotch Reel you are dancing, you Highland fairy?' asked her father. 'Mrs Bretton, there will be a green ring growing up in the middle of your kitchen shortly. I would not answer for her being quite cannie: she is a strange little mortal.'

'Tell Lucy to dance with me, papa: there is Lucy Snowe.'

Mr Home (there was still quite as much about him of plain Mr Home as of Count de Bassompierre) held his hand out to me, saying kindly, 'he remembered me well; and even had his own memory been less trustworthy, my name was so

The Wassail Cup of 'Old October'

often on his daughter's lips, and he had listened to so many long tales about me, I should seem like an old acquaintance.'

Everyone had now tasted the wassail-cup except Paulina, whose pas de fée, ou de fantaisie, nobody thought of interrupting to offer so profanatory a draught; but she was not to be overlooked, nor baulked of her mortal privileges.

'Let me taste,' said she to Graham, as he was putting the cup on the shelf of the dresser out of her reach.

Mrs Bretton and Mr Home were now engaged in conversation. Dr John had not been unobservant of the fairy's dance; he had watched it, and he had liked it. To say nothing of the softness and beauty of the movements, eminently grateful to his grace-loving eye, that ease in his mother's house charmed him, for it set him at ease: again she seemed a child for him – again, almost his playmate. I wondered how he would speak to her; I had not yet seen him address her; his first words proved that the old days of 'little Polly' had been recalled to his mind by this evening's childlike light-heartedness.

'Your ladyship wishes for the tankard?'

'I think I said so. I think I intimated as much.'

'Couldn't consent to a step of the kind on any account. Sorry for it, but couldn't do it.'

'Why? I am quite well now: it can't break my collar-bone again, or dislocate my shoulder. Is it wine?'

'No, nor dew.'

'I don't want dew; I don't like dew: but what is it?'

'Ale – strong ale – old October; brewed, perhaps, when I was born.'

'It must be curious. Is it good?'

'Excessively good.'

And he took it down, administered to himself a second dose of this mighty elixir, expressing in his mischievous eyes extreme contentment of the same, and solemnly replaced the cup on the shelf.

'I should like a little,' said Paulina, looking up; 'I never had any "Old October": is it sweet?'

'Perilously sweet,' said Graham.

She continued to look up exactly with the countenance of a child that longs for some prohibited dainty. At last the Doctor relented, took it down, and indulged himself in the gratification of letting her taste from his hand; his eyes, always expressive in the revelation of pleasurable feelings, luminously and smilingly avowed that it was a gratification; and he prolonged it by so regulating the cup that only a drop at a time could reach the rosy, sipping lips by which its brim was courted.

'A little more – a little more,' said she, petulantly touching his hand with her forefinger, to make him incline the cup more generously and yieldingly. 'It smells of spice and sugar, but I can't taste it; your wrist is so stiff, and you are so stingy.'

He indulged her, whispering, however, with gravity: 'Don't tell my mother or Lucy; they wouldn't approve.'

'Nor do I,' said she, passing into another tone and manner as soon as she had fairly assayed the beverage, just as if it had acted upon her like some disenchanting draught, undoing the work of a wizard: 'I find it anything but sweet; it is bitter and hot, and takes away my breath. Your old October was only desirable while forbidden. Thank you, no more.'

And, with a slight bend – careless, but as graceful as her dance – she glided from him and rejoined her father.

I think she had spoken truth: the child of seven was in the girl of seventeen.

The Great Yorkshire Spice Cake

The origins of Yorkshire Spice Cake, which Charlotte Brontë took to the homes of the parishioners in her father's and later her husband's parish, are lost in the mists of time. Certainly it has connections with York Main Bread, which was well known throughout the county as early as the fourteenth century.

Served with a slice of cheese, the great cake was given to family and visitor alike, and no home would be without it. In *Wuthering Heights* we can read that the grumpy puritan servant, Joseph, left his 'cake and cheese for the fairies.'

Not only in Yorkshire, but throughout Britain, great houses and farms, which supported the local populace, would bake a huge batch of such cakes to give to those who would not have been able to afford the dried fruits and spices necessary to make their own. Parsonages the length and breadth of the country were filled with the rich spicy fragrance, as dutiful wives, daughters and servants prepared the great Christmas cakes. It is the one custom which we can be sure was observed at the Brontë parsonage. The Brontës write about the baking of the cake in several of their novels.

Here is a typical West Riding moorland recipe for Christmas Spice Cake dating from the early 1900s, which will be similar to that prepared by Charlotte Brontë.

2 lb flour
1/2 lb butter
1 lb currants
1/2 lb sultanas
1/2 lb demerara sugar
4 eggs
1/4 lb mixed peel
1 oz yeast
Half a nutmeg
1 teaspoon cinnamon

Crumble the yeast into a little warmed milk. Cover and let rise till frothy. Meanwhile put the flour and two teaspoons salt into a warm bowl. Rub in the butter, then add the risen yeast mix, and the rest of the warm milk, and mix. Cover with a clean cloth and leave in a warm place to rise for 20 minutes. Knead it as you would bread. The more you knead, the lighter the mix will be. Let it rise for a full hour longer, then add the dried fruit and the eggs, which have been well beaten. Mix in thoroughly with your hand. Cover and leave to rise again until double size, about another hour.

Meanwhile prepare cake tins with lining paper, double on the base, and then put in your mixture to about two-thirds. If you want a level top, hollow the mix slightly so that it will rise level and not to a peak. Bake in a well heated moderate oven (160°C) until a knitting needle comes out clean. This takes about 1 hour if you make the mixture into two cakes.

Christmas Customs in Brontë Country

Many of the old traditions which abounded at Christmas time in Yorkshire are steeped in the mists of time, and are no longer found anywhere else. Today, many are forgotten, but there are a few still in living memory, such as the Pretty Box, Vessel Maids and Wassail Bob.

All three of these are related customs, which have developed from one original. That original belongs to pre-Christian times, and was, in fact, an observance in honour of the deity Dionysus. An effigy of the baby Dionysus was placed in a receptacle, and surrounded with pretty flowers and greenery. In the Brontës' Yorkshire, the custom flourished. During Advent, two girls called 'Vessel Maids' would carry round a box, or a double hoop of evergreens with three figures inside: the whole would be covered with a special white cloth which only came out for this purpose – a 'sacred' cloth. The figures now represent the Holy Family.

The box was commonly called a Wesley Bob, a Wassail Bob, a Vessel Cup, a Pretty Box or a Milly Box. People would work very hard at making the decoration around the figures as attractive as possible, with fruits, especially oranges, among the greenery. Various scholars have likened the custom to a pagan rite in honour of vegetation, or a remnant from a medieval Christian crib custom. Others go far beyond and see it as a last vestige of the rites of the child-god Dionysus, and the Vessel Maids – or Vestal Virgins, of course.

The girls, sometimes with an entourage, would carry it from house to house, singing a carol, and asking a penny to see inside, during Advent, the four weeks leading up to Christmas. It was considered most unlucky if the Vessel Maids did not call. So we might be forgiven for presuming that they were expected at the Brontë home, as elsewhere.

The custom adapted and changed; various carols were associated with it: 'The Joys of Mary', 'Here We Come a Wassailing' (noted by Leeds composer, Martin Shaw, whose forefathers had known the custom for several generations). Sometimes there was only one figure, that acknowledged to be the infant Christ Child; sometimes he was accompanied by Mary, occasionally by Joseph too. The Milly Box, a corruption of 'My Lady's Box', usually contained only an image of the Virgin Mary, and the baby would appear on Christmas Day, with new decoration, sugar and spice being added to the other things.

No matter how sheltered from the 'excesses' of Christmas, the Brontë children must have heard the Waits. They were the official city watchmen whose job was to patrol the streets at night and keep the peace. However, as they invariably played musical instruments and/or sang, to show they were on duty, that peace cannot have been kept very quietly! At Christmas time, they played and sang the familiar Christmas carols and songs, and were occasionally rewarded with a few coppers, a pie or a hot drink, it being the season of goodwill.

Carols were also sung at the houses by the choirs of local churches. We have little information about the services held under the Revd Patrick Brontë, the father of the literary family. He had been brought up by an Irish lapsed

Catholic father and a Cornish Methodist mother, and this combination seems to have turned him into something of a bigot. The children, after the death of their mother, were cared for by their aunt Branwell, a strict Wesleyan. Maybe, just maybe, their father's little church sang out with Christmas hymns. The following account of a typical Yorkshire vicarage Christmas is taken from the Leeds Christmas Book by the Director of the Leeds City Museums, P. Brears.

> Probably no Parish Church in England can boast of such a fine musical tradition as that maintained at St Peter's in Kirkgate (Leeds). This is largely due to the work of Dean Hook, the great reforming Leeds vicar.
> When he came in 1837, the church was dilapidated, the surplices in rags and the service books in tatters. By 1841 he had changed everything beyond recognition, the church itself having been handsomely rebuilt, with a new peal of bells and a newly built organ. The quality of the church music was similarly improved, the composer, Samuel Sebastian Wesley serving as organist, and Mr James Hill of Her Majesty's Chapel Royal, Windsor leading the choir of 35 voices. Full choral services were now introduced for all weekday evenings, in addition to those for Sundays and Holidays.

Samuel Dyer was one of the choirboys at this time, and he has recorded the festivities which Dean Hook organised for the choir at the vicarage at No. 6 Park Place.

> 'At Christmas we all dined, men and boys, at the Vicarage: grand for us boys. Plum pudding, Roast Beef, and the games of hunting for sixpences in hillocks

of flour turned out of a basin, or bobbing for apples dangling from a string; after that, presents of knives and books . . . before breaking up we had rounds glees, and madrigals, "Old Thomas Day" and "Great Tom is Cast".
'For several nights about X'mastide, we trudged to the suburban seats to sing outside the mansions of the gentry who frequented the Parish Church, for which we reaped a rich harvest.'

The game with the flour was known as 'Bullet Pudding,' and was, together with apple bobbing, an ancient and well-loved tradition enjoyed by gentry and commoner alike, but sadly, we do not know whether these seasonal customs were followed in the Brontë household.

The Traditional Festive Board

Festive food customs were, and still are, more prevalent in Yorkshire than anywhere else at Christmas. Customs going back many hundreds of years have come down to the modern generation, adapted and modernised many times, but still identifiable with their forerunners.

The Brontë household would have observed many of these customs; indeed they often refer to the pre-Christmas baking both in personal correspondence and novels. Yorkshire, unlike many other regions of Britain, retained the Christmas Eve ceremonies, begun with the ringing of the church bell which ended the Advent fast and abstinence. This custom is found in isolated pockets all over Europe, and is particularly strong still in Poland, although the foods are different.

At around six in the evening, or when the first star appears in the sky, the bells from the churches would announce the end of the abstentions, and the housewife would begin to cook the 'furmenty', a wheat dish which was the main Christmas Eve dish everywhere. Even the ancient Vikings had a wheat dish called 'muga'. All the family gathered together around the table. The new log was placed on the fire, and lit from the brands of the old. Then the youngest girl would light the Christmas candle from the log, and place it on the table. Once lit, all other lights were extinguished, and the meal begun.

Before the meal commenced, a new cheese was brought to the table. In former times this was blessed at church beforehand. The master of the house would cut a cross into the cheese, and say another blessing over it. Sometimes a slice was cut and wrapped in oiled cloth for any member of the family absent from the table.

First eaten was the furment (also known as furmenty and frumenty), which was usually followed by apple pie, then yule cake, spice cake or gingerbread with a slice of the blessed cheese. The wassail bowl was drunk, or sometimes a hot posset made with hot milk and spiced ale, just before going to bed.

Christmas Day began with a groaning board filled with cold pressed meats and brawns, pies and pickles. This cold repast remained throughout the season for any visitor to help themselves. The main meal, for those who could afford it, was a huge goose pie, sometimes with the addition of other game such as hare, rabbit and pheasant. Yorkshire pies were so famous that they were sent to many other parts of the country once the railways made quicker transport possible. During the Brontës' time, papers reported the sending of enormous pies; one, sent from Sheffield to London in 1832, weighed 14 stone but collapsed under its own weight en route!

For those who could not afford this delicacy, the preferred meat was roast beef, served with vegetables. A 'starter' of Yorkshire pudding, served with the gravy from the meat, helped to stretch the joint, as it filled people up before the main course!

Recipe for Furmenty

1 lb kibbled wheat
1 pt milk
1 1/2 oz flour
1/2 teaspoon allspice, nutmeg or cinnamon
2 oz treacle or honey

Mix the flour into the milk, bring gently to boil, stirring, add all other ingredients and bring almost to boiling point. At this stage, currants may be added to taste. Pour into basins and serve hot.

Some older recipes leave the wheat in the milk overnight or for two days to thicken, leaving out the flour. It is then seasoned and sweetened and cooked.

The following recipe for gingerbread was given by an elderly inhabitant of Haworth. She was over 80 back in the 1960s, and remembered a huge batch of gingerbreads being made, and moulded into shapes to give to all the children at Christmas, when she was about 5 or 6 years old. The following recipe belonged to her grandmother, who apparently knew the Brontës very well.

A Good Recipe for Moulded Gingerbread

2 lb good white flour, well-sieved
1 lb tin best black treacle, or 1/2 lb treacle and 1/2 lb syrup
1/4 lb dark sugar
1/4 lb sweet butter
1 teaspoon each of the following: cloves ground; cinnamon; allspice

½ teaspoon of ground anis seeds
6 teaspoons ground ginger
(A lighter gingerbread can be made by using honey and syrup instead of treacle and syrup.)

Melt the treacle, sugar, butter together over a low fire and do not let it boil. Put it to the dry ingredients and knead into a soft dough. Cover with a warm cloth and work close to the fire so that the dough will not go cold. Take small pieces, roll in a mixture of flour and ginger, and press into the moulds that you have well buttered. Turn them out and bake on a baking iron for 3 hours in a medium fired oven.

(Note: This recipe works at 250° F, gas mark 1, or 130°C; if using a modern fan oven shorten the time, and if using a circotherm oven, lower the heat to 120°C after the first hour.)

The Christmas Party

A CHRISTMAS POEM
TOM TWISLETON

This poem is full of the images of a Christmas such as the Brontës would have witnessed. Written originally in Craven dialect, this version has been slightly 'anglicised' for easier reading – with apologies to the author and the fine dialect! Tom Twistleton was born of farming stock, and would have been only ten years old when Charlotte Brontë died.

When cold December's sturdy breeze
In Chimney tops did grumble,
Or, tearing through the leafless trees
On long dark nights did rumble,
A lot o' young folks, smart and gay,
And Old 'uns, free and hearty,
Agreed among themselves that they
Would have a Christmas party
    At home some night.

A merrier lot than this I name
Ne'er met at any party,
All great grand balls they put to shame,
They were so gay and hearty.

Here one had made herself quite fine,
With lace, and braid's assistance;
And there a great grand crinoline,
To keep t'lads at a distance
     Stood out that night.
Against the host o' good things there
They wage an awful battle;
They're crying out, 'A little bit more!'
An' plates an' glasses rattle.
Here, one's no time a word to pass,
Twixt supping and twixt biting;
There, simpering sits a great soft lass
That waits for much inviting
     An' fuss that night.

An' when this good substantial fare
Has given 'em satisfaction,
They side all t'chairs, and stand in pairs,
With heels in tune for action.
See-sawing, the fiddler now begins
The best that he is able;
He rosins his stick and screws up t'pins.
And jumps up onto the table,
     To play that night.
And when they've reeled and danced their fling,
Their chairs all round are ranged;
They tell droll tales, they laugh, they sing,
And jokes are interchanged.
An' merry tune the kettle sings
And t'fire burning brightly;
With cheerful din t'owld farmhouse rings
And hours fly over them sweetly
     And swift that night.

An Imposter at Christmas

CHARLOTTE BRONTË

This is an extract from the fragment of *Emma*, the unfinished last novel written by Charlotte Brontë shortly before she died. The fragment appeared in a copy of the *Cornhill Magazine* in April 1860, in an article by Thackeray, entitled 'The Last Sketch'. One would assume, from the tone of his introduction, as a last tribute to a respected contemporary. Little is known about this story, even the title heroine is a mystery, but the extract here refers to a Christmas at a boarding school for young ladies, such as that which the young Misses Brontë had hoped to open.

One clear winter morning, as Mr. Ellin was seated at breakfast, enjoying his bachelor's easy chair and damp, fresh London newspaper, a note was brought to him marked, 'private' and 'in haste'. The last injunction was vain, for William Ellin did nothing in haste – he had no haste in him; he wondered anybody should be so foolish as to hurry; life was short enough without it. He looked at the little note – three-cornered, scented and feminine. He knew the handwriting, it came from the very lady Rumour had so often assigned him as his own. The bachelor took out a morocco case, selected from a variety of little instruments a pair of tiny scissors, cut round the seal, and read 'Miss Wilcox compliments to Mr. Ellin, and she should be truly glad to see him for a few minutes, if at leisure. Miss W. requires a little advice. She will reserve explanations till she sees Mr. E.'

Mr. Ellin very quietly finished his breakfast; then, as it was a very fine December day – hoar and crisp, but serene, and not bitter – he carefully prepared himself for the cold, took his cane, and set out. He liked the walk; the air was still; the sun not wholly ineffectual; the path firm, but lightly powdered with snow. He made his journey as long as he could by going round through many fields, and through winding, unfrequented lanes. When there was a tree in the way conveniently placed for support, he would sometimes stop, lean his back against the trunk, fold his arms, and muse. If Rumour could have seen him, she would have concluded that he was thinking about Miss Wilcox; perhaps when he arrives at the lodge his demeanour will advise us whether such an idea was warranted.

At last he stands at the door and rings the bell; he is admitted, and shown into the parlour – a smaller and more private room than the drawing-room. Miss Wilcox occupies it; she is seated at her writing table; she rises, and not without air and grace – to receive her visitor. This air and grace she learnt in France; for she was in a Parisian school for six months, and learnt there a little French, and a stock of gestures and courtesies. No: it is certainly not impossible that Mr. Ellin may admire Miss Wilcox. She is not without prettiness, any more than are her sisters; and she and they are one and all smart and showy. Bright stone blue is a colour they like in dress; a crimson bow rarely fails to be pinned on somewhere to give contrast; positive colours generally grass greens, red violets, deep yellows – are in favour with them; all harmonies are at a discount. Many people would think

An Imposter at Christmas

that Miss Wilcox standing there in her blue merino dress with pomegranate ribbon, a very agreeable woman. She has regular features; the nose a little sharp, the lips a little thin, good complexion, light red hair. She is very business-like, very practical; she never in her life knew a refinement of feeling or thought; she is entirely limited, respectable and self satisfied. She has a cool, prominent eye; sharp and shallow pupil, unshrinking and inexpansive; pale iris; light eyelashes, light brow. Miss Wilcox is a very proper and decorous person; but she could not be delicate or modest because she is naturally destitute of sensitiveness. Her voice, when she speaks, has no vibration; her face no expression; her manner no emotion. Blush or tremor she never knew.

'What can I do for you, Miss Wilcox?' says Mr. Ellin, approaching the writing table, and taking a chair beside it.

'Perhaps you can advise me,' was the answer, 'or perhaps you can give me some information. I feel so thoroughly puzzled and really fear all is not right.'

'Where? And How?'

'I will have redress if it be possible,' pursued the lady; 'but how to set about obtaining it! Draw to the fire, Mr. Ellin; it is a cold day.'

They both drew to the fire. She continued:

'You know the Christmas holidays are near?'

He nodded.

'Well about a fortnight since, I wrote, as it is customary, to the friends of my pupils, notifying the day when we break up, and requesting that, if it was desired that any girl should stay the vacation, intimation should be sent accordingly. Satisfactory and prompt answers came to all the notes except one, that addressed to Conway Fitzgibbon, Esquire, May Park, Midland County: Matilda Fitzgibbon's father, you know.'

The Brontës' Christmas

'What? Won't he let her go home?'

'Let her go home, my dear sir! You shall hear. Two weeks elapsed during which I daily expected an answer; none came. I felt annoyed at the delay as I had particularly requested a speedy reply. This morning I had made up my mind to write again, when – what do you think the post brought me?'

'I should like to know.'

'My own letter – actually my own – returned from it the post office, with an intimation – such an intimation! – but read it for yourself.'

She handed to Mr. Ellin an envelope; he took from it the returned note and a paper – the paper bore a hastily scrawled line or two. It said, in brief terms, that there was no such place in Midland County as May Park, and that no such person had ever been heard of there as Conway Fitzgibbon, Esquire.

On reading this, Mr. Ellin slightly opened his eyes.

'I hardly thought it was so bad as this.'

'What? You did think it was bad then? You suspected that something was wrong?'

'Really! I scarcely knew what I thought or suspected. How very odd, no such place as May Park! The grand mansion, the oaks, the deer, vanished clean away. And then Fitzgibbon himself! But you saw Fitzgibbon. He came in his carriage?'

'In his carriage!' echoed Miss Wilcox; 'a most stylish equipage, and himself a most distinguished person. Do you think after all, there is some mistake?'

'Certainly a mistake; but when it is rectified. I don't think that May Park or Fitzgibbon will be forthcoming. Shall I run down to Midland County and look after these two precious objects?'

'Oh, would you be so good, Mr. Ellin? I knew you would be so kind; personal enquiry you know – there's nothing like it.'

'Nothing at all. Meanwhile, what shall you do with the child – the pseudoheiress, if pseudo she be? Shall you correct her – let her know her place?'

'I think,' responded Miss Wilcox reflectively – 'I think not exactly as yet; my plan is to do nothing in a hurry; we will inquire first. If after all she should turn out to be connected as was at first supposed, one had better not do anything which one might afterwards regret. No; I shall make no difference with her until I hear from you again.'

'Very good. As you please,' said Mr. Ellin, and with that coolness which made him so convenient a counsellor in Miss Wilcox's opinion. In his dry laconism she found the response suited to her own outer worldliness. She thought he said enough if he did not oppose her. The comment he stinted so avariciously she did not want.

Mr. Ellin 'ran down,' as he said, to Midland County. It was an errand that seemed to suit him; for he had curious predilections as well as peculiar methods of his own. Any secret quest was to his taste; perhaps there was something of the amateur detective in him. He could conduct an inquiry and draw no attention. His quiet face never looked inquisitive, nor did his sleepless eye betray vigilance.

He was away about a week. The day after his return he appeared in Miss Wilcox's presence as cool as if he had seen her but yesterday. Confronting her with that fathomless face he liked to show her, he first told her he had done nothing.

Let Mr. Ellin be as enigmatic as he would, he never puzzled Miss Wilcox. She never saw enigma in the man. Some people feared, because they did not understand, him; to her it had not yet occurred to begin to spell his nature or analyse his character. If she had an impression about him it was, he was an idle but obliging man, not aggressive, of few words, but often convenient. Whether he were clever or deep, or deficient and shallow, close or open, odd or ordinary, she saw no practical end to be answered by inquiry, and therefore did not inquire.

'Why had he done nothing?' she now asked.

'Chiefly because there was nothing to do.'

'Then he could give her no information?'

Not much: only this, indeed – Conway Fitzgibbon was a man of straw; May Park a house of cards. There was no vestige of such a man or mansion in Midland County, or in any other shire in England. Tradition herself had nothing to say about either the name or the place. The Oracle of old deeds and registers, when consulted, has not responded.

'Who can he be, then, that came here, and who is this child?'

'That's just what I can't tell you: an incapacity which makes me say I have done nothing.'

'And how am I to get paid?'

'Can't tell you that either.'

'A quarter's board and education owing and masters' terms besides,' pursued Miss Wilcox. 'How infamous! I can't afford the loss.'

'And if we were only in the good old times,' said Mr. Ellin, 'where we ought to be, you might just send Miss Matilda out to the plantation in Virginia, sell her for what she is worth, and pay yourself.'

'Matilda, indeed, and Fitzgibbon! A little imposter! I wonder what her real name is?'

'Betty Hodge? Poll Smith? Hannah Jones?' suggested Mr. Ellin.

'Now,' cried Miss Wilcox, 'give me credit for some sagacity! It's very odd, but try as I would – and I made every effort – I never could really like that child. She has had every indulgence in this house; and I am sure I made great sacrifice of feeling to principle in showing her much attention; for I could not make anyone believe the degree of antipathy I have all along felt towards her.'

'Yes, I can believe it. I saw it.'

'Did you? Well it proves my discernment is rarely at fault. Her game is up now, however, and time it was. I have said nothing to her yet; but now –'

'Have her in whilst I am here,' said Mr. Ellin. 'Has she known of this business? Is she in the secret? Is she herself an accomplice, or a mere tool? Have her in.'

Miss Wilcox rang the bell, demanded Miss Fitzgibbon and the false heiress soon appeared. She came in her ringlets, her sash, and her furbelowed dress adornments – alas! no longer acceptable.

'Stand there!' said Miss Wilcox, sternly, checking her as she approached the hearth. 'Stand there on the farther side of the table. I have a few questions to put to you, and your business will be to answer them. And mind – let us have the truth. We will not endure lies.'

Ever since Miss Fitzgibbon had been found in the fit, her face had retained a peculiar paleness and her eyes a dark orbit. When thus addressed, she began to shake and blanche like conscious guilt personified.

'Who are you?' demanded Miss Wilcox. 'What do you know about yourself?'

A sort of half interjection escaped the girl's lips; it was a sound expressing partly fear, partly the shock the nerves feel when an evil, very long expected, at last and suddenly appears.

'Keep yourself still, and reply, if you please,' said Miss Wilcox, whom nobody should blame for lacking pity, because nature had not made her compassionate. 'What is your name? We know you have no right to that of Matilda Fitzgibbon.'

She gave no answer.

'I do insist upon a reply. Speak you shall, sooner or later. So you had better do it at once.'

This inquisition had evidently a very strong effect on the subject of it. She stood as if palsied, trying to speak, but apparently not competent to articulate.

Miss Wilcox did not fly into a passion, but she grew very stern and urgent; spoke a little loud; and there was a dry clamour in her raised voice which seemed to beat upon the ear and bewilder the brain. Her interest had been injured – her pocket wounded – she was vindicating her rights – and she had no eye to see, and no nerve to feel, but for the point in hand. Mr. Ellin appeared to consider himself a strict looker-on; he stood on the hearth very quiet.

At last the culprit spoke. A low voice escaped her lips. 'Oh, my head!' she cried, lifting her hands to her forehead. She staggered, but caught the door and did not fall. Some accusers might have been startled by such a cry, even silenced; not so Miss Wilcox. She was neither cruel nor violent; but she was coarse, because insensible. Having just drawn breath, she went on harsh as ever.

Mr. Ellin, leaving the hearth, deliberately paced up the room as if he were tired of standing still, and would walk a little for a change. In returning and passing near the door, and the criminal, a faint breath seemed to seek his ear, whispering his name –

'Oh, Mr. Ellin!'

The child dropped as she spoke. A curious voice – not like Mr. Ellin's, though it came from his lips – asked Miss Wilcox to cease speaking and say no more. He gathered from the floor what had fallen on it. She seemed overcome, but not unconscious. Resting beside Mr. Ellin, in a few minutes she again drew breath. She raised her eyes to him.

'Come my little one; have no fear,' he said.

Reposing her head against him, she gradually became reassured. It did not cost him another word to bring her round; even that strong trembling was calmed by the mere effect of his protection. He told Miss Wilcox with remarkable tranquillity, but still with a certain decision, that the little girl must be put to bed. He carried her upstairs, saw her laid there himself. Returning to Miss Wilcox he said:

'Say no more to her. Beware, or you will do more mischief than you think or wish. That kind of nature is very different from yours. It is not possible that you should like it; but let it alone. We will talk more on the subject tomorrow. Let me question her.'

There is no more to this last unfinished manuscript of Charlotte Brontë's, and the mystery of the little Christmas imposter must so remain!

A New Year Fête

MRS GASKELL

The following extract is the seasonal chapter from Mrs Gaskell's novel, *Sylvia's Lovers*, published in 1863, just three years before she died suddenly of a heart attack. It shows the casual acceptance of the Christmas preparations and festivities amid everyday life, as it was in the mid-nineteenth century countryside. The story takes up as Sylvia's mother, who has been ill with rheumatic fever, is recovered enough to join the family for Christmas, and the family atmosphere begins to lighten as they realise that she is not going to die. Sylvia appreciates how she would miss her mother, and decides that she will never leave her to marry. This is a blow to Phillip, for whom she is the only girl in the world, and a matter of some disbelief to her neighbours, who proceed to tease her throughout the party she attends, having been persuaded by her mother to go 'a-merry-making' and leave her parents at home by the fire:

At this hour, all the actors in this story having played out their parts and gone to their rest, there is something touching in recording the futile efforts made by Phillip to win from Sylvia the love he yearned for . . . The day before, he had hurried off to Haytersbank Farm with a small paper

A New Year Fête

parcel in his pocket – a ribbon with a little briar-rose pattern running upon it, for Sylvia. It was the first thing he had ever ventured to give her ... He touched it tenderly, as if he were caressing it, when he thought of her wearing it; the briar-rose (sweetness and thorns) – seemed to be the very flower for her; the soft green ground on which the pink and brown pattern ran, was just the colour to show off her complexion. And she would in a way, belong to him ...

Sylvia had made a promise to her mother, and more to herself, that she would not stay late at the party, but she might go as early as she liked; and before the December daylight had faded away, Sylvia presented herself at the Corneys'. She was to come early in order to help set out the supper, which was arranged in the large old flagged parlour, which served as best bedroom as well. It opened out of the house-place, and was the sacred room of the house, as chambers of similar description are still considered in retired farmhouses in the north of England. They are used on occasions like the one now described for purposes of hospitality ...

Sylvia had taken off her hat and cloak by this time and began to help Molly and a younger unmarried sister in laying out the substantial supper.

'Here,' continued Mrs Brunton, 'stick a bit o' holly in yon pig's mouth, that's the way we do things i' Newcassel; but folks is so behindhand in Monkshaven. It's a fine thing to live in a large town, Sylvia; an' if yo're looking out for a husband, I'd advise yo' to tak' one as lives in a town ... '

Bessy saw that Sylvia was annoyed, and with more delicacy than her sister, she tried to turn the conversation.

'That's a pretty ribbon in thy hair, Sylvia; I'd like to have one o' t'same pattern. Feyther likes pickled walnuts stuck about t'round o' beef, Molly.'

'And who might it be as give it thee, Sylvia?' asked the unscrupulous, if goodnatured Molly.

'My cousin Phillip, him as is shopkeeper at Fosters,' said Sylvia innocently...

'Oh, oh! our cousin Phillip is it? ... I've no need to be a witch to put two and two together. He's coming here tonight, isn't he, Bessy?'

'I wish yo' wouldn't talk so, Molly,' said Sylvia; 'me an' Phillip is good enough friends, but we niver think on each other in that way; leastways, I don't' –

... 'There Molly!' said she (Bessy), 'Yo' nivver seed more vittle brought together i' Newcassel, I'll be bound; there'll be above half-a-hundredweight o' butcher's meat, besides pies and custards. I've eaten no dinner these two days for thinking on't; it's been a weary burden on my mind, but it's off now I see how well it looks. I told mother not to come near it till we'd spread it all out, and now I'll go and fetch her.'

As the evening approaches eight o'clock, the old farmer goes off to bed, he suitably catered for by a 2 lb of spiced beef, and a hot tumbler of stiff grog! Leaving his guests to see in the New Year, and partake of his wife's Tea and Supper and praise the magnificence of his bounty. The young people proceeded to get everything in the room ready for the party which would last all the night to see the New Year in. The table holding the immense festive supper pushed back, and the walls lined with chairs ready for the eating, drinking, dancing and playing of old country games. Sylvia determined not to notice Phillip as much as politeness would allow, so as not to give him any encouragement.

They first begin as the guests arrive with tea, and great piles of bread and butter and cake.

When the tea was ended, there was a great bustle and shifting of places, while Mrs. Corney and her daughters carried out trays full of used cups, and great platters of uneaten bread and butter into the back kitchen, to be washed up after the guests were gone . . . Sylvia forced herself to be as active in the service going on as became a friend of the house; and she was too much her mother's own daughter to feel comfortable at leaving all the things in the disorder which to the Corney girls was second nature.

'This milk mun go back t'dairy, I reckon,' said she, loading herself with milk and cream.

'Nivver fash thysel' about it,' said Nelly Corney; 'Christmas comes but onest a year, but if it does go sour; and mother said she'd have a game at forfeits first thing after tea to loosen folk's tongues, and mix up t'lads and lasses, so come along.'

But Sylvia steered her careful way to the cold chill of the dairy, and would not be satisfied till she had carried away all the unused provision into some fresher air than that heated by the fires and ovens used for the long day's cooking of pies and cakes and much roast meat.

When they came back a round of red-faced 'lads' as young men up to five-and-thirty are called in Lancashire and Yorkshire if they are not married before, and lasses, whose age was not to be defined, were playing at some country game, in which the women were apparently more interested than the men, who looked shamefaced, and afraid of each others' ridicule. Mrs. Corney, however, knew how to remedy this, and at the sign from her a great jug of beer was brought in. This jug was the pride of her heart, and was in the shape of a fat man with white knee breeches, and a three-cornered hat; with one arm he supported the pipe in his broad, smiling mouth, and the other was placed akimbo and formed a handle. There was also a great china punch-bowl filled with grog made after an old ship recipe, current in these parts, but not too strong, because if their visitors had too much to drink at that early part of the evening, 'it would spoil t'fun,' as Nelly Corney had observed....

Sylvia was by all acknowledged and treated as the belle. When they played Blind-Man's-Buff, go where she would, she was always caught; she was called out repeatedly to do what was required in any game, as if all had a pleasure in seeing her light figure and deft ways. She was sufficiently pleased with this to have got over her shyness with all except Charley... and now came Crying the Forfeits. Molly Brunton knelt down, her face buried in her mother's lap; the latter took out the forfeits one by one, and as she held them up, said the accustomed formula –

'A fine thing and a very fine thing what he (or she) do who owns this thing?'

One or two had been told to kneel to the prettiest, bow to the wittiest, and kiss those they loved best; others had had to 'bite an inch off the poker,' or such plays upon words. And now came Sylvia's new ribbon that Phillip had given her (he almost longed to snatch it out of Mrs. Corney's hands and burn it before all their faces, so annoyed was he with the whole affair).

'A fine thing and a very fine thing – a most particular fine thing – choose how she came by it. What must she do as owns this thing?'

'She must blow out t'candle and kiss t'candlestick.'

In one instant, Kinraid had hold of the only candle within reach, all the others had been put up high on inaccessible shelves and other places. Sylvia went up and blew out the candle, and before the sudden partial darkness was over he had taken the candle into his fingers, and according to the traditional meaning of the words, was in the place of the candlestick, and as such was to be kissed. Everyone laughed

A New Year Fête

at innocent Sylvia's face as the meaning of her penance came into it, everyone but Phillip, who almost choked.

'I'm candlestick,' said Kinraid, with less of triumph in his voice than he would have had for any other girl in the room.

'Yo' mun kiss t'candlestick,' cried the Corneys, 'Or yo'll nivver get your ribbon back.'

'I'll none kiss t'candlestick, nor him either,' said Sylvia, in a low voice of determination, turning away, full of confusion.

'Yo'll no get yo'r ribbon if yo dunnot,' cried one and all.

'I don't care for t'ribbon,' said she, flashing up with a look at her tormentors, now her back was turned to Kinraid. 'An' I wunna play any more such like games . . .'

As she saw others submitting, quite as a matter of course, to similar penances, she began to be angry with herself for having thought twice about it . . . her eyes kept filling with tears at her isolated position in the gay party . . . Sylvia started a little when Phillip spoke, and kept her soft eyes averted from his after first glance; she answered him shortly, but with unaccustomed gentleness, he had only asked her when she would like him to take her home . . .

'Go home? I don't know! It's New Year's Eve! . . .'

Mrs. Corney, having heard his question, broke in with all sorts of upbraidings. 'Go home! Not see t'New Year in! Why, what should take 'em home . . . wasn't there a moon as clear as day? . . . And were they to break up the party before the New Year came in? And was there not supper with a spiced round of beef that had been in pickle pretty nigh sin' Martinmas, and hams, and mince-pies, and what not?'

The next few hours are taken up with this traditional north-country feast, during which Sylvia and Charley get to know one another better, and Phillip gets more angry as he realises that she does not return his feelings. Seeing his angry glance, she decides discretion the better part, and makes her excuses to go home to her ailing mother, refusing all attempts from Charley to walk her home, and saved from Phillip's attentions by the arrival of her father, who has come early, forecasting that they will all be snowed up well before the New Year is seen in, if they don't break up the party. Once they have gone, Phillip becomes, in Mrs Gaskell's words, 'A wet blanket on the merriment of the party' and he too takes his leave:

The field paths would have been a matter of perplexity, had it not been for the well-known gaps in the dyke side, which showed the whitened land beyond ... at length he was in the lane, toiling up the hill, from which by day, Monkshaven might be seen. Now all features of the landscape before him was lost in the darkness of night, against which the white flakes came closer and nearer, thicker and faster. On a sudden, the bells of Monkshaven Church rang out a welcome to the New Year. From the direction of the wind, it seemed as if the sound was flung with strength and power right into Phillip's face. He walked down the hill to its merry sound – its merry sound, his heavy heart. As he entered the long High Street of Monkshaven, he could see the watching lights put out in parlour, chamber, or kitchen. The new year had come, and expectation was ended. Reality had begun.

He turned to the right where he lodged with Alice Rose. There was a light still burning there, and cheerful voices were heard. He opened the door; Alice, her daughter and Coulson stood as if awaiting him. Hester's wet cloak hung on a chair before the fire; she had her hood on, for she and Coulson had been to the Watch-night.

The solemn excitement of the services had left its traces upon her countenance and in her mind. There was a spiritual light in her usually shadowed eyes, and a slight flush on her pale cheek. Merely personal and self-conscious feelings were merged in a loving goodwill to all her fellow-creatures. Under the influence of this large charity, she forgot her habitual reserve, and came forward as Phillip entered, to meet him with her New Year's wishes – wishes that she had previously interchanged with the other two.

'A Happy New Year to you, Phillip, and may God have you in His keeping all the days thereof!'

He took her hand and shook it warmly in reply. The flush on her cheek deepened as she withdrew it. Alice Rose said something curtly about the lateness of the hour and her being much tired; and then she and her daughter went upstairs to the front chamber, and Phillip and Coulson to that which they shared at the back of the house.

Acknowledgements

The full texts of the extracts used in this book may be found in the following:

'Christmas Correspondence with the Poets' in *The Brontës' Life and Letters* (Clement Shorter, vols I and II, Hodder & Stoughton, 1898), *The Life and Correspondence of Robert Southey* (Cuthbert Southey, Longman, 1850, 1950) and *The Life of Charlotte Brontë* (Elizabeth Gaskell, Haworth edn, Smith Elder, 1900)

'A Wuthering Heights Christmas' in *Wuthering Heights* (Emily Brontë, T. Newby, 1847)

'The Old Man in the Chariot' in 'The Search after Hapiness' (Brontë juvenilia), courtesy the British Library

'An Imposter for Christmas' in the fragment of *Emma* published in the *Cornhill Magazine*, 1860

'A Tragic Tale' and 'The Wassail Cup of "Old October"' in *Villette* (Charlotte Brontë, Smith Elder, 1853)

'A Christmas Remembered' and 'A Ball, Charades and Christmas Baking', in *Jane Eyre* (Charlotte Brontë, Smith Elder, 3rd edn, 1848)

Acknowledgements

'The Brontës at Christmas', 'The Legend', 'Tabby's Ice Accident' and 'The Last Spice Cake' in *The Life* (Gaskell)

'The Islanders' in *The Life* (Gaskell) and *Letters* (Shorter)

'Music on a Christmas Morn' and 'The Cheerful Hearth' in an anonymous manuscript album of Victorian poems in the author's collection; 'December' on a printed page stuck into an album in the same collection

'Christmas Decking', 'The Holly Tree' and 'The Mahogany Tree' in *Christmas with the Poets*, 1842

'Christmas in the Country' in *Hone's Yearbook*, 1827

'The Christmas Critic' in *Fraser's Magazine*, 1844

'The Christmas Party' in *The White Rose Garland*, 1949

'Christmas Storms and Sunshine' in *Howitt's Magazine*

'A Remonstrance against Juvenile Parties' in Punch, 1846

'The Sparkling Bough', 'The Magic Lantern Show' and 'The Music of Pantomime' in *Sketches and Travels* (n.d., 1840s)

'New Year Fête' from *Sylvia's Lovers* (Elizabeth Gaskell, Smith Elder, 1891)

For oven temperature conversions, thanks to NEFF

All unacknowledged work and original research has been done by Maria Hubert in the Christmas Archives Research Library.

Thanks go to the staff of the Haworth Museum; the Keighley Reference Library; the Manuscript Room of the British Library; the efficient and friendly staff of the Monmouth Library; Cardiff Reference Library. And my husband who is my chauffeur, assistant researcher, proofreader and much more, and without whom I would be lost!